A Contemplation of Wine

of Wine

H Warner Allen

T0346426

Published 2021 by Académie du Vin Library Ltd
academieduvinlibrary.com
Founders: Steven Spurrier and Simon McMurtrie

Publishers: Simon McMurtrie and Hermione Ireland
Editor: Susan Keevil
Art Director: Tim Foster
Typesetting: Cheshire Typesetting

ISBN: 978-1-913141-25-7
Printed and bound in the UK

A Contemplation of Wine

H Warner Allen

Introduced by Harry Eyres

ACADEMIE DU VIN LIBRARY • CLASSIC EDITIONS

Académie du Vin Library Classic Editions

In the Vine Country by Edith Somerville and Martin Ross – (1893)

Wayward Tendrils of the Vine by Ian Maxwell Campbell – (1948)

Stay Me With Flagons by Maurice Healy – (1940)

academieduvinlibrary.com

Académie du Vin Library Classic Editions

Our Académie du Vin Library 'Classic Editions' lie at the very heart of the books we publish. When Steven Spurrier and I first talked about a new publishing imprint over lunch at our club (where else!), it was the older wine books we thought of first. These islands have been the heartland of wine appreciation, it seems, since Chaucer's time and there is much literature to draw from: wine writing that is elegant, informative, inspiring, often eccentric and frequently witty. Some of it feels dated now but that's part of its charm. What a shame it would be, we said to one another, if the words that inspired our own wine careers were lost to today's reader. Indeed, they shouldn't be! So while we at the Académie celebrate new authors, new adventures and new perspectives on our pages (and always will), we are now very proud to devote a new series of 'time capsule' titles to the wine writers who handed the job – if you can call it that – over to us.

I have shelves of these books, and quite a few favourites. Here, we welcome back Herbert Warner Allen (1881–1968), who after diligent reporting from the French frontline during World War I became a much-respected wine author and writer of detective novels. It's incredible what you can learn from him.

Hugh Johnson

About the Author

Herbert Warner Allen was born in Godalming, Surrey, in 1881. He was educated at Charterhouse School and won a scholarship to University College, Oxford. His affinity for literature and language (he spoke French, Spanish and Italian) saw him appointed Paris correspondent for *The Morning Post* in 1908, allowing him experience of the French capital as the *Belle Epoque* drew to a close.

Making regular forays to the French and Italian frontlines during World War I, Warner Allen worked special correspondent for *The Morning Post* and *The Daily News*. In 1918 he transferred to the American Expeditionary Force, accompanying it as it occupied Germany. He was made a CBE in 1920 and was awarded the *Légion d'Honneur* for his wartime services. He also served in World War II, surviving a cross-channel flight of the *Morning Post* dirigible.

Herbert Warner Allen is best known as an author of wine books, among them *Gentlemen, I Give You Wine!* (1930) and *The Romance of Wine* (1932), earning the compliment: 'His reader need go in no fear of arrogance.' He was also a successful writer of detective fiction, his adventures often warming to a wine theme – among them *Mr Clerihew, Wine Merchant* (1933) and the short story *Tokay of the Comet Year* (1930). In his collaboration with the novelist E C Bentley, *Trent's Own Case* (1936), an amateur criminologist travels to Champagne as part of a murder investigation. Herbert Warner Allen died in 1968.

Introduction
Harry Eyres

You could read H Warner Allen's delightfully discursive, compulsively rambling *A Contemplation of Wine* as in essence a meditation on changing fashions in wine drinking, and gastronomy more generally. His exceptionally long historical perspective reveals that very few of what we now regard as fairly generally accepted rules in oenosophy (a word Warner Allen likes to use and which should return to currency) and gastronomy applied as recently as the early or mid-19th century. The supposedly great gastronome Jean Anthelme Brillat-Savarin knew very little about the finer qualities of French wines; Edgar Allen Poe didn't realize that amontillado was a type of sherry (though that doesn't take away from the macabre brilliance of his tale *The Cask of Amontillado*, 1846).

What goes for wine also goes for writing. Warner Allen's somewhat ornate style, replete with literary and classical references, is decidedly out of fashion. It might even be described as 'belletristic', a term of abuse when I was studying English literature. But as fashions turn and return, Warner Allen, one of the best-known wine writers of the generation which includes André Simon, seems on rereading to be by no means as fusty and outdated as you (or I) might have assumed. That is despite the fact that something about him remains incurably

Edwardian (he was born in 1881 and died in 1968) and when he speaks of the 'seventies he means the 1870s.

H Warner Allen also led a much more adventurous and varied life than almost any contemporary wine writer I can think of – which is not meant to be a criticism of my colleagues. He was *The Morning Post*'s correspondent in Paris following H H Munro (Saki), and so was able to experience the decadent, sense-obsessed city we know from the novels of Proust and the prints of Toulouse-Lautrec, and a war correspondent in World War I. He co-wrote a detective novel featuring a wine-loving sleuth with his friend Eric Clerihew Bentley, the inventor of the clerihew. He was also something of a mountaineer, who was able to combine the conquest of impressive peaks with the discovery of obscure country wines.

Before I digress too much myself, let me try to get to the heart of what this versatile, hard-to-pigeonhole writer is saying about the subject that most preoccupied him.

A particularly acute and thought-provoking chapter (the chapters are more like essays, freestanding and not directly linked to the ones which precede and succeed them) focuses on the discoveries of the great wine-loving chemist Louis Pasteur, with particular reference to the wines of Jerez and the Jura. Really, this chapter is a meditation on both the achievements and limits of science in relation to wine. He speaks first of the extraordinary hopes which attended Pasteur's discovery that alcoholic fermentation took place as a result of the action of microscopic yeast particles hidden in the bloom of the fruit, announced in 1864. 'It was hoped that human skill and knowledge would now be able to condition the conversion of grape juice into wine, so that grower and producer would be independent of the caprices of weather and geography. The finest wine would be mass-produced, as if its nature were no higher than that of artificial silk or cash registers.' Strangely (to us) this hope was shared by some fine wine producers, such as M Malvezin of Haut-Bailly, who predicted that in future Haut-Bailly 'should have every year the same alcoholic strength, the same breed, the same bouquet'. Of course, nothing of that sort quite happened, though mass production of ordinary wine became vastly more efficient.

Pasteurization of fine wines became common, but has completely fallen from favour. Science, in Warner Allen's view, could salvage mediocre wines, and provide great benefits in regulating and making safer certain processes such as secondary fermentation in bottle, but it couldn't create or guarantee great wines. Only nature could do that, and he keeps harking back to the great and never-equalled sequence of pre-phylloxera Bordeaux vintages between 1864 and 1878.

From here, with a few twists and turns, we reach the Jura, Pasteur's native region, and his researches into *vin jaune* and its kinship with fino and manzanilla sherry. The connection is what is called *flor* in Jerez and *voile* in the Jura. On the track of the microbe that turned wine into vinegar, Pasteur discovered that the *voile* of *vin jaune* was, in fact, a benign organism. This took oxygen from the air and combined it with alcohol, producing a film which protected the wine both from oxygen and the vinegar microbe.

What is most striking here, perhaps, is not so much the undoubted brilliance of the scientist as the fact that cellarmasters, by trial and error at first, but then with careful observation and a 'feel' refined over generations, had found a special way of turning quite ordinary base wines into something bone dry, strange and wonderful.

In the last chapter, Warner Allen enunciates his philosophy of wine, or wine growing, in a way that seems extraordinarily prophetic, and absolutely in tune with contemporary thinking. His ideal is the vigneron (admittedly there is a French bias here) who is guided by the ethical principles he calls *conscience profess-sionnelle*. These include the principle that 'a vigneron worthy of the name [can] only work with, and never against, Nature'. The vigneron must have 'the true connoisseur's love for subtle shades of distinction'. A vigneron of this stamp makes 'wines as an artist paints a picture or a poet pens a poem, not for fame or profit, but for their friends' approval, their own enjoyment, and the satisfaction of their own conceit'.

His exemplar here is a certain M Moreau, a *propriétaire viti-culteur* in Montlouis-sur-Loire, whom he visited on a post-war trip in the late 1940s, a time when he and fellow-Britons were 'cut off from our neighbours by the estranging Channel and an almost impenetrable wall of customs duties'. He came back 'convinced that the art of wine making was very much alive and that there was every hope that good wine would continue to be made so long as our civilization held together'. Beyond that, it 'seemed inconceivable that our two nations should be held apart indefinitely by artificial barriers'. He had a vision, the one originally enunciated by Churchill: 'The union of Western Europe becomes more and more a matter of vital urgency, and what better link could there be than wine.' He would have been delighted to see that vision materialize. What he would have made of the absurdity of Brexit and the return of customs barriers, heaven only knows.

CONTENTS

PART THREE

WINE YESTERDAY AND TODAY: SCIENCE, SHERRY, AND AUSTERITY

AN EPILOGUE ON WINE TOMORROW

The Author's Apology for Omnibibulosity

T HERE is no need, I hope, to apologize for a catholicity of taste in the matter of wine and the other gifts of Dionysus, though it may not be comparable to the all-embracing enthusiasm of Professor Saintsbury. Everything that one has succeeded in enjoying is so much gained, even though its enjoyment runs counter to the laws of aesthetics laid down by the stickler for tradition and hard-and-fast rules. The wider appreciation can be extended, the happier the man of taste, provided that the finer points of artistic beauty are not lost in a too uncritical smacking of the lips. A catholic taste and a capricious memory emphasize, when a man looks back on the pleasures of his life, the importance of the accidental, the surprising effect exercised by conditions and environment on the recollection of an experience which in itself seems scarcely worthy of such vivid representation. The wines that one remembers best are not necessarily the finest that one has tasted, and the highest quality may fail to delight so much as some far more humble beverage drunk in more favourable surroundings. Never the time and the place, said Browning, and the loved one all together. It is amusing to note that when he writes a poem on 'Nationality in Drinks,' the three drinks which spring to his pen are Claret for France, Tokay for Hungary, and beer for England—a selection which one would hardly have anticipated.

Looking back, I must confess that many of the wines that have most impressed themselves upon my memory are not such as would gain more than a contemptuous frown from the connoisseur. I am reminded of a picture in a Tuscan church, which the critic passes by without a word. It has always haunted me because of its setting and because it smiles on the lovely girls who, just married, pray to that Madonna for a son, with the pitying sceptical expression of one who would, but cannot help. True, I have been lucky in tasting most of the greatest wines that fate has bestowed on us during the last century, and have no doubt that the remembrance of the pre-phylloxera clarets will be fresh with me after death. But what stands out is not so much the wines of classical perfection, Château Lafite 1864, Château La Lagune 1858, Château Margaux 1871, and so on, as humbler vintages owing far less to their own merit than to the exceptional setting in which their memory is enshrined.

Certainly 1864 Lafite came to me as a revelation in my undergraduate days. For recollections of far less noble wines I turn to Italy; for without being, I trust, the italianized Englishman of the Renaissance proverb, the devil incarnate, I have always felt the beauty of Italy go to my head and lend to its wines a glamour not their own. Drink generously of the white wine of Orvieto and then contemplate the fantastic façade of the Cathedral that J. A. Symonds calls 'a wilderness of beauties,' and study within the glory of Signorelli's frescoes. So I found myself translated into a world of unearthly form and colour like a dream of heaven and had a glimpse into the intricate loveliness which must form a poet's mind—such a poet as he who wrote:

> As one enamoured is upborne in dream
> O'er lily-paven lakes 'mid silver mist
> To wondrous music.

I have often thought that the regular consumption of

alcoholic refreshment should be compulsory for all dull, humdrum folk, and that only poets, musicians, and other artists should be exempt from this obligation, assuming—which seems improbable—that they wish to be abstainers.

Certainly it would be hard to find a greater proof of Saintsbury's catholicity and unconventional courage than the good word he finds to say for the much-abused Green Muse, absinthe. He finds all the ceremonial and etiquette which make the proper fashion of drinking it delightful to a man of taste, and certainly to the eye the clouding of the emerald into ethereal opal and to the taste 'the extra-ordinary combination of refreshingness and comforting character in odour and flavour,' compose 'a very agreeable experience.' He tells us that after rough handling by the ocean absinthe picks one up as nothing else will, and I can add from experience that one of the most delightful sensa-tions that life can provide is the savour of a dash of absinthe in the water carried in the guide's gourd, when, after a mighty struggle, one has conquered a mountain peak. Those who experiment with it will do well to remember that it has the curious property of doubling the effect of every drink that is taken after it, so that half a bottle of wine at the meal which follows it will be equivalent to a whole bottle.

The mention of climbing, in the last paragraph, recalls to me a Swiss wine which has remained fresh in my memory rather as a curiosity than for its excellence. Civilization has, I fear, claimed the Val d'Anniviers, which its inhabitants used to boast was the most primitive valley in the whole of Switzerland. Already when I knew it many years ago, they were fettering its headlong torrent, the Navigenze, and enclosing its waters in enormous pipes for base factory uses. There at a wedding feast, under pine forests rising to the Alps' eternal snow, I tasted the food and drink traditional for such festivities. Among the viands, an ancestral cheese held the place of honour. For such an occasion, it had been

9

preciously preserved for a hundred years, and old age had made its exterior all gnarled and nobbly. Its consistency was that of hard wood and its flavour strong rather than agreeable to the unaccustomed taste, but it was most highly thought of and needed vast quantities of wine from Sierre in the valley below to wash it down. The wine in which the bride's health was drunk was reputed as old as the cheese. For it came from a family cask which was called upon to play the part of the small army of casks that form the Solera of an established sherry. For over a hundred years it had never been completely emptied, and it contained only wine of the choicest vintages. Its age was proved by a deposit as hard as limestone which lined it inches deep, so deep that there was little space left for the wine. On great occasions it was drawn upon, but never to a greater extent than two-thirds of its contents, and it was refilled to the bung with the best of the recent vintages. It was an interesting experience to taste that wine and that cheese, but there was a bitterness about them both which only the natives could find agreeable. The wine was all salt and metal, like unblended centenarian sherry, and had that extreme dryness and bitterness, though perfectly sound, which Pliny attributes to the wines of the Opimian vintage of 121 B.C., the most famous vintage in wine history—*vina usque in amaritudinem carie indomita.*

There is nothing bitter about my youthful memory of a wine at which in later life, I fear, I should have turned up my nose, describing it as sugar and soda water or something equally rude. Yet I doubt if any drink I ever tasted produced equally exquisite sensations and contentment. On the hills above Alassio, on the Italian Riviera, there is a little col where two views meet: on the one side the blue Mediterranean with a line of snowy Apennines on the horizon, and on the other the landward view, the enchanted valley of Albenga. It was a glorious climb to reach it, up precipitous *salite,* mule paths, which wound their way through the olives. In the early March sunshine there would still be patches of snow lying on the upper slopes, and the cool breeze blowing from the Alps challenged the laziest climber to press onward to the summit, the Madonna della Guardia. It must be nearly fifty years since I last scaled those heights, and there are twists in the path which I can still see as distinctly as if I had trodden them yesterday.

In the valley beneath there lies the village of Moglio, and in it is a little inn built in Spanish style round a *patio*. The inn-keeper grows his own wine, and on the way up the climber should ask him for a bottle of his Moscato, specifying that it must have been pressed from the grapes grown on the southern slopes of his vineyards. (Once it cost just one lira.) Consigned to a knapsack, that bottle should make the ascent on the purchaser's shoulders. I can still see the rock, like a lion couchant, which just below the Madonna della Guardia throws into the shadow a patch of snow, where the bottle can be buried in cold white refreshment, while the rest of the climb is accomplished in the swiftly-increasing warmth of the spring sun. Thence one could plunge head-long back to the enjoyment of that gay little wine, with its faint sparkle like a young Moselle and its sweetness corrected by a touch of acidity, and feel as one's thirst was quenched, that all was for the best in the best of all possible worlds. For fear of spoiling that memory, I have never dared touch Italian Moscato again and never will.

I must conclude with a recollection in utter contrast. Port, the Professor tells us, should never be asked to act purely as a thirst-quencher, and he tells the sad story of ladies who had been playing lawn tennis in the garden of Professor Goldwin-Smith being invited by their host to quench their thirsts. 'After a few minutes, during which the damsels naturally became thirstier than ever, their host reappeared, bearing on a mighty silver salver glasses of—port wine! They were not so ungracious as to refuse it; but it did not exactly meet their views.'

11

Such a contretemps befell Lester Lawrence and myself a quarter of a century ago when we were walking on Exmoor. Soon after noon, when we had covered at least a dozen miles over the moor from 'The Stag Hunters,' at Brendon, we came to Simonsbath, very hot, very thirsty, and avid for refreshment. Our hopes were high, for the map—I have it yet—marked Simonsbath as possessing hotels in the plural, a wealth of entertainment very rare in the almost inn-less Exmoor Forest. As we went down the steep descent to the little town, we passed a horseman and asked him the way to the nearest inn. His reply nearly broke our hearts. There was nothing at Simonsbath that he could call an inn; for there was not a licensed house in the place. He was riding out to get his daily glass of beer at Exford, five or six miles away. Murmuring something about Port which we did not understand, he saluted us and rode on in thirsty haste.

We came to a place that was half-hotel, half boarding-house, and our request for liquor was curiously countered by the reply that, as they had no licence, they could offer us no beverage but Port. Sadly we agreed to accept whatever they might have, and Port they brought us. After one sip, we fell back on water with as thankful a heart as we could muster; for that Port holds high rank in my memory as one of the nastiest potions that ever passed my lips. Perhaps it was a local brew of elder and whortle berries, but ordinary elderberry wine would have been nectar compared to it.

PART ONE

Three Portraits
by way of
Dedication

I

A Gourmet of Time Long Past: Brillat-Savarin

ANTHELME BRILLAT-SAVARIN lived in a world not at all unlike our own; for he cultivated the art of Good Living with the fabric of civilization cracking, crashing and collapsing under the strains and stresses of the French Revolution. He knew the pangs of exile, and fond as he was of the good things of this life, there came to him a revelation of the spiritual truth that lies behind them; asceticism has no monopoly of the grace of mysticism. Here, however, we are concerned with him under his self-conferred degree as Professor of Gastronomy. For us his lectures open with a queer and challenging note. 'Water is the only beverage that effectually quenches thirst, and it is for this reason that it can only be drunk in very small quantities.' Whether this remark is to be regarded merely as a statement of fact or as a warning to the reader of *La Physiologie du Goût* not to be careless and waste a beautiful thirst by over-indulgence in Adam's ale I do not know. In the matter of liquid refreshment, the great classic of gastronomy is lamentably lacking in philosophic guidance and artistry; he defends himself on the ground that his Meditation on Drinks is purely theoretical, since if he had entered into detail there would have been no end to it.

15

There is a want of conviction and consistency in his comments on wine, and he administers a shock to the wine-lover when he finds a good word to say in favour of that unholy institution, High Tea. Writing in 1825, he says: 'Sugar, coffee, tea, chocolate, alcoholic liqueurs and all the consequent combinations have converted good cheer into a composite whole, in which wine is nothing but a more or less optional accessory; for tea is an excellent substitute for wine with a meal.' The English and Dutch, he adds, in a footnote, eat bread, butter, fish, ham, and eggs, and hardly drink anything with them but tea. Surely the greatest gourmet of all time can only be thinking of breakfast; he uses the word *déjeuner*, which elsewhere in his book certainly means lunch, since in one case it consisted of two dozen oysters for each guest, kidneys *à la brochette*, a terrine of truffled *foie gras*, and that very substantial Swiss dish, a *fondue*, made on the table by Brillat-Savarin himself, a savoury mess of buttered eggs and cheese. One is thankful that he did not insist on his guests, two aged cousins, washing down this meal with tea, but gave them two bottles of Sauternes—which I am sorry to say he spelled without the final *s*—and, as he kept them to dinner, reserved tea for the conclusion of that meal, much to their surprise; they were old-fashioned folk and regarded tea as a medicine. We are not told what wine was drunk at dinner, but even though Brillat-Savarin did not insist on his guests swallowing High Tea, his heresy cries out to Heaven for vengeance when he belittles fermented juice of the grape into 'a more or less optional accessory.'

In truth, the aesthetics of wine were in their infancy at the beginning of the nineteenth century. One searches in vain through the masterpiece of this Professor of Gastronomy, as he styled himself, for a vintage year or the discussion of aroma or bouquet. Once or twice he throws some light on the wines he thought particularly good, but only by accident. Thus he looks up the word *Gourmandise* in the dictionary and is distressed to find that it is always confused with gluttony and voracity. He concludes that lexicographers, estimable people as they no doubt are, do not belong to the class of attractive scholars who partake so gracefully of a supreme of partridge and, with finger elegantly crooked, raise to their lips a glass of Lafitte [sic] or Clos Vougeot to wash it down. He mentions the comet of 1811 and the great heat ascribed to it, but he says nothing of that historic vintage, the Opimian vintage of modern times. To read him, one would think that a sweet liqueur should be regarded as artistically superior to the finest wine. Evidently the French gourmets of the time had not got over the sensational novelty of sweetened alcohol.

Our Professor of Gastronomy is more interested in the sugar-cane and beetroot than in the vine. It is true that he tells us the little story of the drinker who refused grapes on the ground that he was not in the habit of taking his wine in the form of pills, but he devotes pages to sugar with an enthusiasm which reminds us that it had only just become a necessity instead of a rare luxury. In the middle of the eighteenth century it was discovered that sugar similar to that brought in from the cane of the Indies could be extracted from beetroot, and Brillat-Savarin assures us that in his time there were not ten out of a hundred Englishmen who would believe it. A little macabre in his tastes, he had an idea that sugar might be valuable for embalming corpses in view of its preservative qualities instanced in jam and so on. The mixture of sugar with alcohol, the basis of the liqueurs invented to warm the old age of Louis Quatorze, was at that time regarded as the most delicious of all conceivable tastes, thanks to the grip of the alcohol on the palate and the exquisite perfume offered to the olfactory sense. The passion felt for sugar is illustrated by a man of letters who complained that sugar cost over five francs a pound. Brillat-Savarin quotes him as saying in a voice of tender yearning: 'If only sugar came

17   B

down to thirty sous, I would drink nothing but sugared water.'

Again our gourmet lets himself go on chocolate, named by Linnaeus *cacao theobroma, the beverage of the gods,* advises his readers to buy their chocolate at M. Debauve, *Chocolatier* to the King, 26 rue des Saints-Pères, and quotes a recipe for its making from the Mother Superior of a convent at Belley, his home, which ends with the pious reflexion that 'the good God could not take offence at the little refinements introduced to make it excellent, since He Himself is all excellence.'

Brillat-Savarin is no doubt beyond reproach in the general principles of his gastronomical philosophy, though he lived in an age of gross feeding—the exiles of the French Revolution tried to make up for lost time when they found themselves back at home—and the niceties of Oenosophy made little appeal. Wine was taken for granted in a way that we can hardly understand in this country today, though doubtless when this island had its own vineyards and its own *crus,* we should have grasped the inner meaning of the tale concerning the wine of that Paris suburb Suresnes. It was said that it took three men to drink a glass of Suresnes, one to drink, the other two to hold the drinker up and prevent him from losing courage. In spite of the prevailing vinous Philistinism, which allowed tea to be mentioned in the same breath as wine, *The Physiology of Taste* lays down for all time two of the fundamental rules concerning the presentation of both food and drink. No. XI of Brillat-Savarin's twenty Maxims ordains that in eating one must proceed from the more substantial to the lighter dish, and the following Maxim declares that the precedence of beverages opens with the lighter and less heavy and ends with the wines of fullest body and richest bouquet. Nowhere in his work can we find any distinction drawn between white and red wines as to their function in a meal, and it is clear from a contemporary number of the *Almanach des*

18

Gourmands, published in 1825, for which the famous connoisseur Grimod de la Reynière was responsible, that the
distinction universally recognized in our days was then
quite unknown. Nothing is said about the incompatibility
of fish and red wine, nor is any attempt make to provide
dishes that will set off the qualities of the finest wines
offered at the feast. Paul de Cassagnac in *Les Vins de France*
quotes from the *Almanach* mentioned above a chapter entitled 'A Journey round a Cellar.' We learn that the half-
and-half connoisseurs, that is hosts of modest fortune, adopt
as their ordinary wines those of Orléans, Auxerre, Joigny,
Coulanges, Vermanton and the other *crus* of Lower Burgundy, and the common wines of Bordeaux. Connoisseurs
take as beverage wines Mâcon, Moulin-à-Vent, the second
qualities of Beaune, the Thorins wines, some red Champagne wines, or the third qualities of Bordeaux. While just
a very few, very rich, past masters in the art of wine drinking, actually serve as ordinary wines, the finest Beaune,
Volnay, and the clarets of Graves and Saint Emilion.

These beverage wines, for the most part probably the
bourgeois *crus* of Bordeaux, and the excellent light wines
of Mâcon, Beaujolais and Chablis were served promiscuously with the first service, which in one meal quoted by
Brillat-Savarin consisted of a huge sirloin, a fricassee of
chicken, a joint of veal and a stuffed carp. First may have
come the *pot au feu,* and we are told that the well-advised
gourmet follows the soup with a glass of dry Madeira.
Brillat-Savarin remarks that this glass of Madeira was an
innovation introduced by Talleyrand in 1801, at the same
time as he brought in the fashion of taking parmesan
cheese with the soup. The second service which in the
meal quoted above was composed of a turkey, a pike, and
six entremets including macaroni cheese, brought in the
finer wines, the first growths of Beaune, Pommard, Clos
Vougeot, Chambertin, or at the guests' choice the second
growths of Bordeaux, Saint Emilion, Château Margaux,

19

and Graves, which are passed round swiftly to prepare for the next course. It is interesting to note that Clos Vougeot and Chambertin are regarded as on a level with the second growths of Bordeaux as well as Saint Emilion, Graves no doubt including Haut Brion, and curiously enough Château Margaux. All such wines are of the second order heralding the finest wines with the third service that consists of vegetables, pastries and more entremets. These wines which should form the crown of the feast are named Bordeaux-Lafite, Romanée, Hermitage, Côte Rôtie, or if white wine is preferred, white Bordeaux, Sauternes, Saint Péray and so on. 'Rudimentary, lacking both method and judgment,' says M. de Cassagnac, and we are bound to accept his verdict. One does not know whether the guests drank indiscriminately one after the other Lafite, Romanée, and the Rhône wines, if they did not prefer Sauternes, but it is surely barbarous to lump all these so different *crus* together. The third service with its vegetables seems to us the most unsuitable course of all for the presentation of great wine— all the more so if some of the entremets were sweet as they probably were—and no palate could form any opinion worth having on the relative merits of a wine list which jumbled together the Rhône, Burgundy, and Bordeaux. The modern taste would certainly not admit Saint Péray as quite in the running with the great Sauternes. Saint Péray has a natural sparkle, which has led to its being dressed up in the robes of Champagne, but as a still wine it may be taken to rank with the Pouilly of the Mâconnais.

After the third service came the dessert, and as part of it consisted of cheeses it seems to us a pity that the great wines were not served at this moment, allowing the sweets to come after with the usual cavalcade of dessert wines, Port, Malmsey (Madeira), Jurançon (near Pau), Malaga, Muscat, Rota Tent (now a sacramental wine), Cyprus and Tokay. It was only at the end of all this that there came the turn of Champagne of the sparkling variety. Red

Champagne—no doubt it was not made so well as the late M. Paillard's Bouzy rouge—had been served as a beverage on the same level as the bourgeois *crus* of Bordeaux, and we may assume that the Champagne which provided the final touch was sweet. Brillat-Savarin makes some remarks about Champagne that seem to lack his habitual shrewdness, but they are interesting in showing that it was not unknown in France at the beginning of the nineteenth century to drink Champagne throughout a meal. He says that Dr. Corvisart, who was Napoleon's doctor and had something of Abernethy's reputation for rudeness, drank nothing at a medical banquet except iced Champagne. At the beginning of the meal when other guests were too busy eating to talk, he was noisy, talkative and full of stories. By dessert when general conversation had woken up, he was serious, silent, not to say cross. 'Champagne,' says the Professor of Gastronomy, stating a theorem as he calls it, 'is exciting in its first effects and stupefying in its later ones, in other words it acts exactly like the carbonic acid gas it contains.' Brillat-Savarin would scarcely win a first prize for acuteness of observation on the strength of this comment.

He picks a bone with the medical profession on the ground of the 'useless' prohibitions the doctors impose upon their patients, and asserts that in 1815 when the Paris hospitals were full of invalids from the allied armies, the ration in wine of a sick Russian would have intoxicated a market porter and that of an Englishman would have more than satisfied that proverbial drunkard, the Limousin. He tells the story of a Canon Rollet, 'a drinker after the manner of days gone by,' who fell ill, and the doctor at once cut off his wine. Next time the doctor called, he found his patient in bed, but before him was spread a table with a nice white cloth, a crystal goblet, a most attractive-looking bottle, and a napkin to wipe his lips. Aesculapius was furious and was threatening to throw up the case, when the unhappy Canon wailed, 'You forbade me to drink, but you never said I must not enjoy the pleasure of seeing the bottle.' Another of Brillat-Savarin's friends was condemned to what he calls the worse fate, not merely of abstinence from wine, but drinking water in large doses. The patient took one mouthful from a great tumbler of water brought him by his wife and gave her back the glass saying, 'My dear, take it and keep it for another time. It never does to play the fool with medicine.'

Water enters again into the Prince of Gourmets' lucubrations when he discusses the use and abuse of finger bowls. About forty years before, he tells us, that is before the Revolution, some people in the highest society, mostly ladies, used to wash out their mouths after they had finished a meal. They left the table and turned their back to the company. A lackey presented a glass of water; they took a mouthful and spat it out into a bowl, and that was the end of it. A new fashion had been introduced, and Brillat-Savarin thoroughly disapproves of it. At the end of dessert, each guest has set before him or her a bowl of cold water with a goblet of hot water standing in it. The fingers are rinsed in the cold water; a sip of the hot water is taken into the mouth and after noisy gargling spat forth—*an innovation as useless and unbecoming as it is disgusting*. It is useless because the mouth should be perfectly clean at the end of a meal, washed out by the juice of the fruit and the final glasses of wine that go with the dessert. It is bad eating to dirty one's hands, and besides there is always a napkin to wipe them with. The French Revolution did not sweep away napkins, and it never occurred to Brillat-Savarin that in the coming century universal war would produce, temporarily at least, a napkinless world.

Nor did he imagine that the day would come when young men would comb their hair and women young and old make up their faces and manicure their nails shamelessly in public conveyances. For him it was a fundamental principle of good manners that ablutions and all operations of the toilette should be conducted in the privacy of the closet. Gargling in public was positively indecent! Finally, how disgusting! When applied to such base uses the prettiest and freshest mouth loses all its charms, and the less said about mouths that are not so pretty and so fresh the better.

In these days of austerity, it is consoling, if a trifle invidious, to read of the banquets that Brillat-Savarin enjoyed, not only after Napoleon had fallen and the Monarchy had been restored, but as a young man when the *ancien régime* was tottering to its fall. He tells of a day spent at a Cistercian monastery near his home at Belley, when he as the leader of an amateur orchestra was invited to come and make music in honour of Saint Bernard. They were young men, and on their arrival found a meal suited to the appetites engendered by a long mountain scramble; for the monastery was high up in the hills at Saint Sulpice. As Brillat-Savarin expresses it, they found awaiting them a *pâté* as big as a church, bounded on the north by a large joint of veal, on the east by a monumental pyramid of butter, on the south by an enormous ham, and on the west by a vast mound of globe artichokes. There was a great variety of fruit, and in one corner of the refectory a stack of more than a hundred bottles, which were kept cool by a fountain playing on them. They attacked the viands set out, but though they did their best, they produced little effect on their abundance. Then as they had been climbing all night, they went to bed and slept, until they were called for mass.

They played a symphonia for the offertory, sang a motet at the elevation of the Host, and wound up with a wind quartet. Then came the time for dinner, which we learn was served after the style of the fifteenth century, few entremets or kickshaws, but a fine choice of meat, simple stews and perfect cooking, while the vegetables had such a flavour as those bought in the market never have. The second service comprised no less than fourteen roasts, and the coffee was particularly good, served in deep bowls from which the pious fathers drank with a noise of whales blowing before a storm.

There was more music at vespers, and the festival ended with a supper which in its delicate refinement belonged to a period several centuries later than the dinner that preceded it. Finally the call went up for the cellarer to present his contribution. It took the shape of what our author calls a veritable vat of burning sugared *eau-de-vie*, probably *marc*, which took the place of punch, a liquor that the fathers had not heard of. It seems a hot night cap for a summer night—the feast of Saint Bernard is on August 20th—but they all slept well and woke refreshed.

Brillat-Savarin was possessed of a gastronomic optimism and a belief in the potential power of Science to appeal to taste and appetite, which has been knocked out of us by recent experience. He concludes *The Physiology of Taste* with a chapter which he calls an 'Historical Elegy'; it consists of a lively recital of the advances made in the Art of Good Living with the progress of civilization and dwells on what each age missed by being born too soon. He starts with Adam and Eve who sacrificed salvation for an apple and wonders what they would not have done for a truffled turkey, if only there had been cooks in the Terrestrial Paradise. He drops a tear on the Homeric heroes who were doomed never to know the refinement of a fricassee of chicken, and pities those lovely Greek ladies who for all their beauty never tasted a meringue. The Vestal virgins might have been reconciled to the horrible fate of being buried alive that awaited them when they had been naughty, if only they had enjoyed the delicious syrups and preserved fruits of a later age, while the Roman financiers who held the world in fee had no conception of the charm of ice-cream. The Paladins again, after their feats of heroism, never received from the hands of a lovely dark-eyed captive a glass of sparkling Champagne, or Malmsey of Madeira, or luscious liqueurs, the invention of the Golden Age of the Grand Monarque; the best they could hope for was beer or sour wine. The Templars were deprived of the joys of chocolate and coffee, and the wives of the crusaders, who promoted their pages to conjugal rank during their husbands' absence at the wars, never shared with their paramours a biscuit or macaroon. Brillat-Savarin winds up by condoning with his contemporaries, the epicures of 1825, who would never know the wonders that science was preparing for them in 1900. He did not choose the date badly, though science had little to do with the gastronomic excellence of the early twentieth century. Fancy dishes made from minerals such as he foretold were, thank heavens! still unknown, and there had been no sublimation of liqueurs through atmospheric pressure. Indeed, anticlericalism was about to banish from France the greatest of all monastic liqueurs which after 1903 was to be produced at Tarragona. But he was right in his anticipation that there would be such an importation of delicacies from all parts of the world into Europe as had never before been seen. What a different tale there would have been to tell if he had fixed on a date forty odd years later!

Never were the Paris restaurants more prosperous and famous than at the end of the nineteenth and beginning of the twentieth century, when they had recovered their pristine glory of the Second Empire. Brillat-Savarin dates the establishment of restaurants from about the year 1770; previously visitors to Paris had to depend on the inn-keepers whose cookery was usually bad. Up to that time, according to the Prince of Gourmets, the men of wealth and power had had the exclusive enjoyment of two advantages: they travelled fast, and always ate well. They lost the first advantage with the institution of public carriages that travelled fifty leagues in twenty-four hours, and the second with the establishment of restaurants which put the best of fare within everyone's reach. Anyone who had from fifteen to twenty francs to spare could eat as well at a restaurant as at a prince's table. There follows a vivid description of a restaurant of the day from which I extract a single paragraph: 'Here and there foreigners are to be seen, mostly English. They stuff themselves with double helpings of meat, call for everything that is most expensive, and drink the most heady wines, often needing to be helped from their table.' One thing the Englishman of today can claim, though he could do with double helpings; he does not ask for the most expensive dishes, because if he did he would not be able to pay for them with a Treasury-regulated purse, and, perhaps we may add that, if he does like a wine of body, he is usually quite capable of leaving his seat without an arm.

Gastronomy, it seems, profited greatly from the foundation of restaurants, since as soon as it was discovered that the invention of a new dish might make a cook's fortune, a deal of ingenuity was expended on the kitchen. The tendency for meals to grow dearer as dishes became more and more *recherché* was countered by the *restaurant à prix fixe*, which, while making a profit of between 25 and 30 per cent, provided an adequate meal for two francs or even less, quite good enough for a gentleman—*tout homme bien né*—who would have to spend at least a thousand francs a month to keep up at home a table as plentiful and varied.

The most famous restaurateur of Brillat-Savarin's time and a pioneer in the business was Beauvilliers, who made and lost fortune after fortune and prospered mightily during the occupations of Paris by the Allies in 1814 and 1815. He had a marvellous memory and never forgot a face. He showered attention on his rich customers, advising them not to take one dish, to make haste and order another, and recommending yet another that no one had thought of, arranging for wine to be brought from the inmost cellar of which he alone kept the key. It almost seemed as if all these extra attentions called for no extra charge. Then Beauvilliers disappeared, and when the bill came the price of his attentions was only too apparent.

There was an abundant choice of food in the great restaurants of Brillat-Savarin's time. The customer could select from twelve soups, from fifteen to thirty entrées of beef, mutton, poultry or game, and veal respectively, to say nothing of twenty-four dishes, fifteen roasts, fifty desserts and so on. When we come to the wine list the choice seems more restricted. Brillat-Savarin speaks of thirty varieties of wine from Burgundy to Tokay and Constantia with between twenty and thirty kinds of liqueurs besides coffee and such mixed drinks as punch, negus, syllabub, and so on. Thirty wines to over twenty liqueurs seem to us quite disproportionate, but the French at that time were hypnotized by the all too obvious fascination of sugar, scent and alcohol in the newly-invented liqueurs.

It was *gourmandise*, the art of good living in food and drink, which enabled France to pay off the indemnity of 1,500,000,000 francs imposed upon her in 1815, a sum that seemed in those unsophisticated days astronomical beyond computation, though it would do little more than pay for our National Health Service for a year. The occupying armies were not long content with the rations which the defeated country was required to provide. 'They gorged themselves on meat, fish, game, truffles, pastry, and fruit. Their thirst equalled their appetite and they perpetually demanded the most expensive wines, hoping for some unheard-of delight that they never found. Superficial observers did not know what to make of this unending eating and drinking without thirst or hunger, but the thoroughgoing Frenchman laughed and rubbed his hands, saying: "They are bewitched and by tonight they will have paid us back more than the public Exchequer paid them out this morning." ' Brillat-Savarin tells us in a footnote that when the invading armies passed through Champagne they took 600,000 bottles from the cellars of M. Möet of Epernay, who was reconciled to his loss when he found that the wine commandeered had served as an advertisement and that his orders from the north were more than doubled.

The world in those days had no memory of such a period of general peace as that before the first World War and was far more hardened to the exigencies of war than we are today even after a second World War. Brillat-Savarin talks lightly of the occupation of Paris, because he himself has memories of occupying enemy territory in Napoleonic days. He was on Marshal Augereau's staff in Germany, and the staff officers complained that they had neither fish nor game. They were right, says Brillat-Savarin; for it is a maxim of equity that the conquerors should make good cheer at the expense of the conquered. So he wrote to the Head Forester and explained politely that they wanted fish and game. That official was an old soldier who loathed the French, and he replied that all his keepers had run away, the floods made it impossible to catch fish, and so on. Brillat-Savarin made no reply except to quarter ten grenadiers on the Forester. Two days later there arrived a waggon load of venison, woodcock, carp, pikes and so on, enough to keep the Staff in luxury for a week. The grenadiers were withdrawn and the Forester gave no more trouble.

We see the gourmet at his best when the Terror was at its height, and even the shadow of the guillotine could not blunt the zest of his appetite for a good meal. He was riding his good horse *La Joie* through the Jura on his way to Dôle with the slender hope of persuading a revolutionary official to give him a safe-conduct that would save him from prison and its probable sequel, the scaffold. About lunch time he stopped at a village inn, and after he had seen to his mount, his eyes met a most delightful spectacle. Over the kitchen fire was roasting a spitful of quails, king quails, and beside them a nice fat leveret. Full of hope, he asked the landlord what he could offer, and was overwhelmed with disappointment at the reply that there was soup, shoulder of mutton and beans. None of these dull dishes were to the liking of an epicure, and our author persuaded mine host to tell the party which had shot the game that a good companion would like to join them and pay his share of the bill. They were legal experts who had been valuing confiscated property in the neighbourhood and were celebrating the end of their labours. One of their number came down and had a look at Brillat-Savarin and evidently thought that he looked a good sort of chap, as he was invited to join them. He skipped upstairs to their private room and the meal and company were up to his expectations; the trouble he had had in getting within reach of the game heightened its flavour. They drank a *vin rosé*, perhaps Tavel, followed by Hermitage, and finally *vin de paille*, sweet wine of dried grapes, with liqueurs of Verdun to follow. Brillat-Savarin forgot all about the guillotine, as he says with pride, and improvised a catch that he trolled to the company amid general applause.

They were eating for four hours, and the westering sun warned him that he must go on with his journey, though the others implored him not to go. They were careful to ask no indiscreet questions—people in those days were shy of showing uncalled-for curiosity—but he made it clear to them that his ride was not exactly a pleasure trip. He came safely to Dôle and found the revolutionary official anything but agreeable; indeed, he seems to have been on the point of having him arrested. It was not, says Brillat-Savarin with remarkable detachment, that he was a bad fellow, but he was not very intelligent and had no idea what to do with the terrible power of life and death that had suddenly come into his hands. He was like a baby with the club of Hercules. However, the arrest was postponed after explanations and the official whose name was Prôt was persuaded with difficulty to come and have supper with a mutual friend. There again he looked very sourly at Brillat-Savarin, though his wife gazed with interest at this candidate for the guillotine.

'Do you like music?' was her first question.

Brillat-Savarin could have cried with joy; for he was the keenest of amateur musicians. She had been a professional teacher of singing and had had no opportunities of discussing her favourite subject. So they talked operas, composers and musicians to their heart's delight, until, after supper, Mme Prôt sent for her music. 'She sang,' writes our author, 'I sang, we sang; never did I put more feeling in my voice or sing so well. Her husband wanted to leave, but she would not hear of it, and we wound up like a couple of buglers sounding the charge with the duet from *La Fausse Magie: Vous souvient-il de cette fête?*'

As she left, Mme Prôt said: 'Citizen, lovers of the fine arts like you cannot be traitors to their country. I know you want something from my husband. You shall have it. I give you my word.'

Brillat-Savarin kissed her hand with untold fervour, and next day received his safe-conduct duly signed and magnificently sealed. So he went home rejoicing with his head on his shoulders, and, as he put it, thanks to Divine Harmony, that beloved daughter of Heaven, his ascension to her abode of bliss was postponed for quite a number of years.

II

A Wine-Lover of Yesterday:
Professor George Saintsbury

I NEVER had the honour of meeting Professor Saintsbury in the flesh, but half a century has passed since
he first became to me a very real and living personality.
When I was at Oxford in the first years of this century, my
best friend Francis Tower Gray, had been one of Saintsbury's favourite pupils at Edinburgh University. Gray and
I saw a great deal of one another, so much so that a wag
coined the portmanteau name of Grallen to cover us both
on the ground that we were unthinkable apart, and
Saintsbury's pupils were never tired of talking about him.
So I heard a great deal of Saintsbury lore, and in particular
I remember an evening made memorable by the Professor
and a great Claret.

My friend was the nephew of the Edinburgh physician
Dr. Bell, who was famous for applying to his patients the
deductive method applied by Sherlock Holmes to criminals,
and who was the actual model of Conan Doyle's classic
detective. That evening he had just been to Scotland where
he had enjoyed the Professor's hospitality. I rather think
he had been one of the guests at the dinner numbered IX
among the menus appended to *Notes on a Cellar-Book*, in
which Château Latour 1893 was the crown of the feast. I

know that we had been drinking a '93 Claret with our meal as preparation for a wine of which I was inordinately proud.

In my last year as an undergraduate, when I was dead broke, as all fourth-year men were in those unregenerate days, I led myself into temptation one afternoon and dropped in at Jones's, the wine-merchant's in the High. A wily salesman with a reverend white beard made a casual remark that there was just one dozen of 1864 Lafite left in the cellar. I was tempted and fell. One hundred and twenty shillings a dozen seemed in those days a fantastic price to pay even for the best Claret the world has ever seen. This wine was reposing under my window seat in the recess which was the nearest approach to a cellar in my digs, when certain sons of Belial, flown with insolence and wine, paid me a visit as they were wont to do, and, finding me out, hunted round for something to devour. Some of them helped themselves to whisky as was right and proper, but more enterprising members of the gang explored the cavity below my window seat. To this day I shudder to think of what followed. They laid sacrilegious hands on my best Claret, and when I came in I found them drinking Château Lafite 1864 out of tumblers with no better excuse than that it seemed to them quite decent red ink.

I had decanted one of the surviving bottles of that precious Claret for Gray and myself that evening when he discoursed on Saintsbury's hospitality. We were enjoying that incomparable wine after the table-cloth had been removed from the polished table, true to the Professor's dictum that the time to appreciate the finest wine comes when the more prosaic and vulgar business of eating is over and done with.

There is nothing to be added to Saintsbury's own account of his own hospitality in *Notes on a Cellar-Book*, and so there would be little point in repeating my friend's account of that dinner, even if I remembered it. What I do remember is how he tried to show me Saintsbury as the man and critic he was by quoting one of his comments on the famous poem by Herrick that opens with the lines:

> Bid me to live and I will live
> Thy Protestant to be.

'I have no idea,' Saintsbury used to say, 'what *Protestant* means in this connection, but I am quite sure that it is the right word in the right place.' These words presented him to me as a hater of humbug and a critic eminently gifted with the soundest common sense, and as such his image has always remained in my mind.

After the First World War, I was brought into personal contact with Professor Saintsbury by correspondence, and, when he wrote some articles for the *Morning Post*, learned that he was to be numbered among the world's major cacographists. At the *Morning Post* the palm for bad writing had been awarded to Andrew Lang, and all his articles were set up by a special compositor who was regarded as *the* expert in difficult hands. When Lang was out of town, if this compositor was away on holiday, the usual weekly article had to be held over till the printer came back, as no one else could made head or tail of what it was all about. When Saintsbury's manuscript came in, after one glance I sent it up to that same compositor, who boasted that anyone who could decipher Andrew Lang could read any script. Some hours later he came down to see me, a broken man, confessing that in an article about 1,500 words long there were at least twenty words that had absolutely baffled him. When Saintsbury received a proof with twenty-odd blanks in it, he wrote back a letter, which, so far as we could read it, was lavish with compliments to our printers for having sent him the cleanest proof he had ever known. His handwriting was execrable, but his typing was even worse; for he seemed to strike the keys of his typewriter at utter haphazard, and there was no clue at all to what his arbitrary groups of unassorted letters might stand for.

I have pleaded guilty to the crime of omnibibulosity, and perhaps in his universality I may find an excuse for my error. It may be that his appreciation and sympathies both in wine and literature were a trifle too all-embracing. No doubt in this age of mass production fastidiousness should be our watchword; yet there is a great deal to be said for the ancient Jewish maxim, that on the Judgment Day every man will be called to account for every good thing that he has failed to enjoy, when he could legitimately do so. A Cambridge historian of English literature says of Saintsbury: 'His foible of omniscience is so transparently ingenuous as to be attractive rather than offensive,' and worthily lauds the immense vitality of his enjoyment, that magnificent zest of life, which endeared him to all who knew him. As in letters, so in wine, and it is to be remembered that he boasted never to have given a second-hand opinion either on wine or book.

III

A Deipnosophist of Today:
André Simon

IT was my good fortune to be invited to the dinner given
in honour of André Simon's seventieth birthday and so
to be able to add my mite of appreciation to the con-
gratulations offered on that occasion to the pioneer who
ranks as First Deipnosophist of the British Isles. February
28, 1877, was the day honoured by his birth. I should like
to think that he was born under the constellation of Bacchus, but the Wine God does not seem to be one of the
signs of the Zodiac, and those watery creatures Pisces
appear to be in the ascendant at that time of the year. I
am glad to learn from Whitaker that in astronomical truth
the Pisces have long ceased to exercise any authority over
André Simon's birth date; for the relation between the
calendar and the Zodiacal sign has been completely upset
by the Precession of the Equinoxes during the last two
thousand years. I wonder what the astrologers do about
it! One of the guests who drank Simon's health suggested
that in view of his quite unseemly youthfulness he must
have made a mistake about the date and that he had
been born on February 29th, in Leap Year, so that
having only one birthday in four years he was still in his
teens. It did not seem to strike him that if he was right,

we should all have been deprived of a very good dinner that night.

In those days one hesitated to use the words *good dinner*. There were tales current of a Food Ministry Gestapo watchful for evidence of the lightest rationing peccadillo. We English are a strange people, so ready to carry the best advice to extravagant extremes. Told to love our enemies, we love them so dearly that we are prepared to hate our friends. Fair play, we all know, is a jewel, and our enthusiasm for equality of sacrifice goes so far that it becomes dog-in-the-manger jealousy. If there is not enough of a good thing for everyone to have a share, no one shall have any. If the general cannot have caviare, then there shall be no caviare. The supreme example of the green-eyed monster, punished in Dante's Purgatory by the sewing down of the eyelids, was given in the fuel crisis by the lunatic order, afterwards cancelled, which forbade a man to make use of his water-driven electric power for fear his neighbours should be jealous of him. In our day the wise virgins of the parable would have been fined for hoarding, and the oil they had thoughtfully provided for their lamps would have been distributed among the foolish.

Even now when there is a slight relaxation of austerity, I shrink from distinguishing between the reality of the meal enjoyed at a restaurant by some twenty guests, and those dreams of the culinary art called up by the presence of the Arbiter of Good Living. One cannot be too careful in these days of retrospective legislation. There was certainly Champagne, or so it seemed, Pommery 1928 from a Jeroboam, with an invigorating fillip to distract one's attention from a coalless and freezing world; but was it in a vision that I seemed to be aware of the caviare that calls up for the true Left-Winger the dictatorship of the proletariat? Again I heard someone mention Strasbourg, and instantly there flashed across my palate what might have been a recollection of *pâté de foie gras*, that rich and succu-

36

lent pabulum, from which it had been so long divorced. No doubt it was mere imagination, but how very pleasant!

The next wine was Château Margaux 1929 from a Magnum, following an excellent soup *crème forestière*. I need not say that I was profoundly shocked to hear a fellow guest assert that the soup was so good that he suspected that some real cream had insinuated its way into its composition. Perish the thought! In *Vintage Wise* Simon has proclaimed his faith in the 1929 Clarets as of the class of the '75's and 1900's, putting Mouton at their head. After the mediocrity of Concession wines, Margaux 1929 shone gloriously, though it hardly rose to the eminence of the great vintages mentioned by Simon. Certainly the wines of this vintage have turned out far better than we expected, when they seemed prematurely sweet and agreeable. The Margaux had that suggestion of a hard kernel, *grain* I think is the French word, which promised long life and much improvement to come. There was a saddle of lamb that melted in the mouth, and very pleasantly it combined with first, Domaine de Chevalier 1926 from a Magnum, and then Cheval Blanc 1924 from a similar bottle. The Domaine de Chevalier was a surprise. It was amazingly soft and had so little of the pebbly straightforwardness of Graves that it seemed almost flabby. In point of fact it was delightful, with a charming bouquet, and Simon remarked not without astonishment that he really preferred it to the Margaux 1929. The Cheval Blanc 1924 was well provided with the virtues of its clan and was quite seductive, but somehow I can never remember so well the beauties of Saint Emilion when they have found themselves side by side with the subtleties and delicacies of Médoc. For the next wine, Cheval Latour 1899 in its Magnum was a real beauty. Colonel Ingham Clark tenderly supervised its reception by his fellow-diners as though he had an almost paternal interest in its good behaviour, and he had every reason to be proud of it. No Claret of 1899 that has come my way has preserved so perfectly its dignity and sweetness as this Latour 1899.

While we were being borne away on the wings of this glorious Médoc to the days when good wine was in very truth a familiar creature, I began to dream again. There appeared before my gastronomical eye a noble Brie, big as a fine, round tea-table, and thick with creamy lusciousness. Of course it can only have been a dream, born by wishful thinking out of mouse-trap. Long years ago we thought it rather a joke to make W. H. Smith as a first-rate newsvendor First Lord of the Admiralty, and Gilbert immortalized him in that office as ruler of the 'Queen's Navee.' It is presumably on the same principle that the Government selected for high advisory position at the Food Ministry— W. H. Smith and Gilbert would both have fainted at the extravaganza of such a Department—a lady who does not know the difference between good and factory cheese. It made my blood run cold to read how she had talked about acquired tastes in connection with famous cheeses, as though there was something dishonest about them. She was evidently under the impression that a man has to *acquire* a taste for the native cheese of his locality, though he certainly absorbs it with his mother's milk. The difficulty is not to acquire a taste for Stilton, Camembert, Brie, or Blue Vinney, but to persuade oneself that the ignoble mixture worthily nicknamed mouse-trap is fit to eat and to bring oneself to swallow for the sake of nourishment the emulsions extracted, one could almost think, from train grease or the oil of a motor-car sump. Thinking of the tragedy of cheese I enjoyed the more that imaginary and unctuous Brie, which blended so happily with the great wine of Pauillac.

With the choice of coffee there came a brandy of Simon's birth year, 1877, not indeed a famous vintage year for Cognac, but an excellent Grande Champagne, Hine's. André Simon junior told us how he had discovered in Cognac the shippers themselves drinking this brandy and had persuaded them by the happy coincidence of the date that a Magnum of Hine's Grande Champagne 1877 must be devoted to the celebration of the Septuagenary of his father, always a devoted admirer of the firm's products.

This seventy-year-old brandy set me thinking about birthdays and vintage years. One of my earliest recollections of André Simon—maybe fifteen, maybe twenty years ago—takes me back to his birthday, when he gave me Chambertin 1877 to drink his health, and tried to prove to me that salmon cooked in red wine went perfectly well with red Burgundy or Bordeaux. I still rather shrink from the combination. There is a great deal to be said for being born in a good vintage year and for regularly celebrating one's birthday with a coeval bottle. André Simon is certainly lucky in having started his life with a first-class Burgundy year—he still talks of Musigny 1877, drunk in 1917, with bated breath—and, as for Bordeaux, the 1877 vintage produced some fine wines, though rather of the Peter Pan order, never quite growing up. Usually there was a suspicion of greenness in their farewell, though I have the happiest recollections of a Margaux and Mouton of that year. All wise wine-lovers arranged to be born before the phylloxera. How wise was Colonel Ian Campbell, when he elected to be born in 1870 and to emulate the Clarets of that vintage by growing better and better every year he lives. He could luxuriate in the magnificent Ports of his birth-year, to say nothing of Burgundies by no means to be despised, and legendary Cognacs.

Horace seems to have been fortunate in his birth-year, 65 B.C.; for he was very proud of the Massic made when he was born and Lucius Manlius Torquatus and Lucius Aurelius Cotta were consuls. When he was proposing to make a night of it with that eminent statesman, soldier and man of letters, Corvinus, he was full of confidence in its mellowness and maturity after thirty-five years in the *amphora*, ranking it among those wines which he and Ovid call *languidiora*.

If one had to be born after the phylloxera, what was the

use of 1881, the writer's birth-year? Port was probably the best; 1881's ranked as fair with a few good specimens. Claret was hopeless in full phylloxera. 1899 and 1900 were the only years for younger men to be born in. Looking back over my ancestors, I note that my great grandfather, the greatest wine-bibber of the family, was born in 1782. I do not know whether the year was good or bad, nor do I know whether it had yet become the custom to lay down a pipe of Port when the son and heir was born. If it had, that pipe was certainly laid down, but one pipe would not have carried him very far through his long life; for he was a mighty trencherman and his appetite left its mark on his figure. I have just been reading a letter of his written in the 'sixties, when conundrums were as popular as puns, asking my father why the Rector of Iden (that is himself) was like a nation at war, with the answer, 'because he is belly-gerent.'

I know not what wines Fate may have provided for my maternal grandfather who was born in 1800, but what one has heard of Waterloo Ports is reassuring for the paternal grandfather born in 1815. 1842 ministered to my father's needs some fine Port and poor Claret, and my son, born in 1916, looks out upon a sorry prospect, born too late into a world too old.

So, congratulating Simon on having been born into a better pre-phylloxera world, I transcribe with tears in my eyes the following sentences from his *Art of Good Living*: 'Like all arts, the art of good living has known many vicissitudes. Like all arts, the art of war excepted, it needs peaceful and prosperous times to attain any degree of perfection. During war . . . the mere fact of keeping alive is so grim a business that few, if any, have the means, even if they had the inclination, to cultivate the art of good living. . . . The practice of the art of good living means giving daily the same amount of time and thought to our daily food and drink that we give daily to the question of dress.' *O tempora! O mores!*

40

PART TWO

WINE
and
Yesterday's Seven Thousand Years

Argive Helen's Cocktails and Nestor's Tokay Essence

A WINE-LOVER, writing in praise of wine, might veil his face in shame when he admits for the cocktail, the crude mixed drink that marks the reaction to griping iced water, a semi-divine origin and Homeric immortality, if his better feelings were not armoured in the triple bronze of omnibibulous catholicity. As it is, he cannot deny that to all appearances golden Helen, the daughter of Zeus, did mix for Telemachus and his friend Peisistratus, oppressed by grief, something very like a primitive cocktail of which, alas! the secret has been lost. We do not know what were the bitters, alcohols and liqueurs, the magic drugs from Egypt, which the most beautiful woman ever known mixed in the glass to stay all pain and strife and bring forgetfulness of every evil, but what would we not give for that potion which brought with it such well-being that 'whoso should drink it, not all that day would he let a tear drop down his cheeks, no, not though his father and mother should lie dead before him, nor though before his face men should put to the sword his brother or dear son and his own eyes behold it'?

There may be some doubt as to whether Helen's Gloom Raiser was drunk before the meal, at the cocktail hour, which the modern clock strikes in place of the more roman-tic *heure verte* of the last generation. Telemachus and his companion who had come to Lacedaemon seeking news of Odysseus had eaten on their arrival at Menelaus's palace, and it is not clear how long a time elapsed before golden Helen came down from her fragrant high-roofed chamber as lovely as Artemis of the golden arrows to mix the Nepenthe cocktail which may have served as a prelude to a late supper.

The Roman cocktail-drinker defended his addiction by the Homeric example, and Pliny was certainly of the opinion that the Nepenthe potion was drunk before the meal. 'To drink fasting,' he writes, 'is a new and very un-desirable fashion for people engaged in important business and those who have to keep their wits about them. Wine was taken, no doubt, in ancient times, on an empty stomach, but for the sake of sleep and repose from worries; so in Homer, Helen serves it before a meal.' He goes on to say that the fashion was introduced about forty years before he wrote, during the reign of the Emperor Tiberius, and that it came to Rome from abroad—much as cocktails have come to England. 'Forty years ago when Tiberius Claudius was Emperor, the habit of drinking on an empty stomach and taking wine regularly before meals came in, an out-landish fad recommended by doctors who are always trying to advertise themselves by some new-fangled idea.'

Odysseus at any rate had no truck with cocktails. There were no bitters or alcohols added to the sweet Maronean wine, dark red and of a most amazing strength, which put Polyphemus at his mercy and enabled him to escape from the Cyclops' cave. One measure of that glorious wine from Thrace in twenty measures of water retained such a mar-vellous bouquet that no one could resist it. 'A fragrance would arise from the mixing bowl miraculously sweet; then verily one would not choose to abstain.' Its perfume seems to have belonged to the same supernatural order as

Hera's ambrosial oil, a drop of which would fill heaven and earth with its scent and which Zeus found quite irresistible. Small wonder Maro, the priest of Apollo, who gave it Odysseus, kept that wine for himself and his wife and allowed no servant other than his housekeeper to know of its existence; small wonder too, that Polyphemus was knocked out by three bowls of it neat.

A more interesting wine, the Pramnian, plays a part both in the Iliad and Odyssey. Its supernatural virtues belong to the fairy-tale of Aeaea, Circe's magic island. When Odysseus' companions had heard Circe's sweet voice as she sang before her loom and went into her palace, she beat up for them cheese, barley meal and yellow honey with Pramnian wine, and therewith mixed baneful drugs that they might utterly forget their native land. Then when she struck them with her wand, they were turned to swine.

Apart from sorcery, Homer evidently regarded Pramnian as a wine of the rarest properties. One might say that Tokay Essence—if its continued existence is compatible with dialectical materialism—corresponds to the Homeric panacea, though one would scruple to subject it to the barbarous treatment given to Pramnian in Homer. It is nice to think that some progress has been made since the siege of Troy in spite of the internal combustion engine, poison gas, and atom bombs, and that our refusal to mix wine with cheese, barley meal and yellow honey definitely proves that we have attained a higher degree of civilization.

Pramnian may or may not have been a geographical appellation. The scholiasts suggest that it was made at several different places, and Homer throws no light on its origin. A familiar passage in the Eleventh Iliad describes how Nestor bore out of the battle in his chariot Machaon, son of Asclepius the peerless leech, who had been wounded in the shoulder by an arrow from Paris' bow. Homer shows us the two Greek heroes, standing on the shore and drying the battle sweat from their tunics in the sea-breeze. 'And thereafter they went into Nestor's hut and sat them down on chairs, and for them fair-haired Hecamede mixed a potion. . . . She first drew before the twain a table fair with feet of cyanus and well polished, and set thereon a bronze basket, and therewith an onion, a relish for their drink, and pále honey and ground meal of sacred barley; and beside them a beauteous cup, that the old man had brought from home, studded with bosses of gold; four were the handles thereof and about each two doves were feeding, while below were two supports. . . . Therein the lovely woman mixed a potion for them with Pramnian wine and over it she sprinkled goat's milk cheese with a brazen grater and white barley meal, and bade them drink when she had prepared it. Then when they two had drunk and banished parching thirst, they took delight in tales, telling them one to the other.'

No one but a wine-lover could have described so truly the joy of relaxation and liquid refreshment after the heat of the battle. If the modern connoisseur makes reserves as to the suitability of Nestor's golden goblet for wine, we know at least that its artistic workmanship was probably worthy of its contents; for Schliemann unearthed just such a goblet at Mycenae. We may shudder at the onion as a relish to the Pramnian and have our doubts as to the cheese and barley meal, but there could be no better tribute to the drink which gladdens the heart of man than the picture of the two tired warriors, their thirst quenched, forgetting their fatigue in the joy of telling one another stories. Probably Machaon did not have much chance of working off his best stories on the garrulous Nestor.

This passage has gained additional fame by being quoted by Plato in the Third Book of the *Republic*, all the more because Plato has made a slip in his quotation. He confuses the Machaon episode with another incident in the same Iliad, when Patroclus eased a wound in Eurypylus' thigh by rubbing into it a bitter root, 'a root that slayeth pain.' However, the mistake makes no difference to Plato's argument, which is one that modern doctors are just beginning to take seriously. Hecamede's potion, which in his opinion was distinctly heating for a wounded man, he takes as an example of the rough-and-ready methods of the ancients who either killed or cured and did not keep useless people alive to be a misery to themselves and others.

In classical time there were many speculations as to the nature and origin of Homer's Pramnian wine. According to Athenaeus, it may have been grown in Lesbos, Icaros, another Aegean island, or near Ephesus. Otherwise it may derive its name from a Pramnian vine and merely stand for any dark, long-lived wine. If it be permissible to ignore a fragment of Aristophanes, quoted by Athenaeus, which suggests that Pramnian was neither sweet nor thick, but hard and dry, 'contracting both the eyebrows and the bowels,' its precious qualities seem to be reasonably explained by Dioscorides, a Greek physician, who lived in the first century A.D. He preserves the tradition that it was what the Greeks called *protropon* or *prodromon*, that is, wine made from the minute quantity of juice squeezed out of sun-dried grapes by their own weight before they are trodden. If Dioscorides is right, the Pramnian grapes must have been left on the vines until they were practically raisins as for the Tokay Essence in a good year when the Essence is being made, or possibly they may have had ten days' sun-drying on mats, as Hesiod prescribes. Pramnian wine would thus seem to be the Homeric version of that wonderful restorative, Tokay Essence.

The attar of grapes that oozes like syrup naturally from the very ripe fruit is exceedingly rich in sugar and is a concentration of all the virtues of the grape. It is very rarely fermented apart from the juice forcibly extracted—Tokay Essence was said to be unique—and its rarity is not surprising, since the quantity of wine produced is insignificant in quantity and its price prohibitive. The extreme sweetness of the attar must makes fermentation very slow

47

indeed and owing to the great sugar content only a minimum of alcohol—often under 3 per cent—is formed. Consequently, so far as its alcohol was concerned, Homer's Pramnian was probably less heating than Plato supposed. It would, moreover, fit in well with Athenaeus' description: 'a thick and very nourishing wine prescribed not as *a cure for thirst* but rather to fill the belly.' There is more substance and solidity about Tokay Essence than any other wine. The most benighted teetotaller could not deny it the quality of food, if by accident it crossed the barrier of his teeth, and its consistency and flavour have an odd distant suggestion of brown bread and butter.

If the alchemists in their quest of the Aqua Vitae, the elixir of immortality and eternal life, had chanced across Tokay Essence or any other Pramnian substitute, they might well have believed that they had come very near to the object of their search. Just as a pound of attar of roses represents the fragrance of two tons of rose petals, so a spoonful of Tokay is a compendium of all the virtues, both sensory and restorative, all the vitamins mysteriously created by hours of sunshine, all the properties of strength and rejuvenescence, which form the quintessence of the divine blood of the grape.

I have proved by experience that Tokay Essence is an unequalled restorative. Its effects are instantaneous and magical, as remarkable in their beneficent way as Circe's black magic, and worthy of Nestor's Pramnian and its startling powers of recuperation, though I should deprecate beating it up with anything, even cheese, meal, or onions. My aunt, aged ninety, was dying of bronchitis, and the doctors pronounced her case desperate. They allowed her to have Tokay Essence of 1811 administered in teaspoonfuls and for two days she had nothing else. On the third morning, she was clamouring for breakfast, was out of danger, and lived to miss her centenary by six weeks. She is but one case out of many known to me. It is a tragic thought that the Tokay vineyards lie behind the Iron Curtain.

II

The Vines and Wines
of Ancient Rome

IN a famous passage of the Second Georgic, Virgil embarks on a catalogue of the vines known in his day and brings it to a sudden end in unaffected despair. 'The same vintage does not hang from our vines, as Lesbos gathers from the Methymnean stock. There are Thasian vines as well as the white Mareotic, the one better suited to a heavy, the other to a light soil. The Psythian grapes are best pressed as raisins for dessert wine, and the Lageos, for all its seeming lightness, will make your legs fail beneath you and tie your tongue. There are purple grapes and early-ripening grapes, and how, *cépage* of Rhaetia, shall I praise thee, though thou canst not challenge the vintage of Falernus? Then there are the Amminean grapes with their full-bodied wines, in whose presence the Tmolian vine must rise in reverence and even that king of grapes the Phanaean. As for the little Argitis, nothing can vie with it either in the quantity or longevity of its production. Nor must I pass over the Rhodian, which the gods love and which goes so well with dessert, or Bumastus with its great swelling clusters. But the varieties of the vine and the names of its grapes are beyond number.' Even in Virgil's days they were as countless as the grains of sand swept by the west wind across the Sahara, or the waves of the Ionian sea driven on the Italian shore by an easterly gale.

Pliny gives a list of a hundred names or so, and is content to leave them as 'innumera atque infinita.' Democritus, the globe-trotting philosopher whose conceit knew no bounds, actually claimed to know the name of every vine grown in Greece—and Pliny remarks that this was just like his cheek. Botanists may be able to tell us whether there is any plant which rejoices in such profusion of varieties and local names. Many years ago, long before the phylloxera, the gardens of the Luxembourg contained fourteen hundred varieties of the French vine, and the collection was far from being complete, while at the same period it was computed that the French kinds did not form more than a twentieth part of those grown in Europe. Add to this multitude all the varieties of the American vine, the names of which would have little interest for the wine-lover, if it had not been for the phylloxera. That curse has given their stocks a special value in Europe as bearers of European grafts, since their roots are practically immune against its ravages.

Legion was the name for the multiplicity of vines already known to the ancient Romans, and Legion was also the name of their wines. Virgil has more to say about vines and their culture, and the art of wine-making lies outside the province of the Georgics, so that his scholastic editors run less risk of committing technical blunders in their notes than those who are called upon to deal with the actual process of fermentation and the treatment of the finished article. A taste for wine often goes with a taste for the Classics, and it is a disappointment to one who loves them both to observe how scurvily the commentators often deal with the vinous problems raised by their authors. It is distressing to find an Oxford Don and Editor of Horace, translating *vafer* as *connoisseur*, when it is used of a man who has been blending the wine of Sorrento with Falernian lees, and must surely mean *a faker*.

A casual study of the *Epigrams* of Martial with a special eye for references to wine—they are full of them—brought me to the following odd commentator's note: 'Wine was supposed to suffer some diminution in bulk from being kept long. It was considered also to grow thick and require straining.' Apparently he had never heard of an ullage, or, for that matter, evaporation, and it was probably news to him that wine did sometimes throw a sediment as it aged. The note referred to the following lines:

> Defluat et lento splendescat turbida lino
> Amphora centeno consule facta minor.

Martial proposes to open his best wine to welcome a friend back from Taormina and, to put it prosaically, calls on the amphora ullaged by a hundred consulships, that is a hundred years, to pour forth its contents *candle-bright* when the sediment has been removed by the slowly-filtering muslin. I fear that such wine, however old it may be— and Martial's hundred years no doubt was a figure of speech, as Sir Willoughby Patterne's 'a wine aged ninety' should have been—would have small appeal to the modern taste. It is nothing that it should have been ullaged. As Dr. Middleton said, 'Old wine, my friend, denies us the full bottle!' but this muddiness and slow-filtering muslin arouses the worst premonitions.

The question arises, how did the Romans decant their wines?—and to the best of my knowledge, we have very little information on the matter. How did they get the liquid out of a huge vessel like the *amphora*, holding three dozen bottles and generally terminating in a base which needed to be propped up by a stand or embedded in cement, if it was to stand up straight, and there is no suggestion of the *amphorae* being binned away. In the wine shops, they used to be chained up to a pillar, often intruding on the

51

pavement. Obviously there could be no tapping of an earthenware receptacle or drawing off the wine from beneath. Probably there were few changes in the traditions of keeping and drinking wine during the centuries that followed the downfall of the Roman Empire, and Saint Augustine's mother Monnica seems to have ladled up the wine with a cup from the top of the *amphora* to pour into a decanter, when her family sent her to get the wine for a meal. It will be remembered that she used to treat herself to a sip or two from the cup, and was cured of the habit when the maid who looked after her called her a naughty little drunkard, with the charming diminutive *meribibula*.

It is hard to see why Martial's wine, however old it might be, should be muddy, if it was taken from the top of a newly-opened *amphora*, though it was likely enough that the earthenware vessel would have lost a good deal of wine through evaporation. The true connoisseur did not approve of straining and filtering; at least, Horace tells us that Massic loses its aroma if it is passed through muslin. There is a good deal of evidence that the Romans did bottle their very finest wines in glass bottles much smaller than the *amphorae*. Petronius, Nero's Arbiter Elegantiarum, in his famous description of the banquet given by a vulgar upstart and millionaire, Trimalchio, says that glass *amphorae* were brought in, carefully sealed, and with labels round their necks inscribed 'Opimian Falernian. A Hundred Years Old'. Petronius no doubt intended the label to be humbug, on the lines of Napoleon Brandy, since if the Falernian had belonged to the immortal Opimian vintage 121 B.C., which for its loud-trumpeted longevity threw our Comet Year of 1811 into the shade, it would have been nearer a hundred and fifty than a hundred years old. Martial too talks of Falernian of the Opimian vintage being laid down in small glass bottles. The Speyer Wine Museum used to have a third-century Roman glass bottle, which, apart from two rudimentary handles reminiscent of the 'ears' of the *amphora*, was of surprisingly modern shape and could easily have been binned away. It was not so used, as when it was placed in a sarcophagus some seventeen hundred years ago, oil was poured into its neck to protect the wine from air, just as is done with the Chianti flask. How effective oil is as protection was proved by it having formed a solid cake, hermetically closing the bottle and preserving even to our time a solidified extract of wine which the chemist had no difficulty in analysing.

'Some find sepulchral vessels containing liquors, which time hath incrassated into jellies. For besides these lachrymatories, notable lamps with vessels of oils attended noble ossuaries; and some yet retaining a vinosity and spirit in them, which, if any have tasted, they have far exceeded the palate of antiquity. Liquors not to be computed by years of annual magistrates, but by great conjunctions and the fatal periods of kingdoms. The draughts of consulary date were but crude unto these, and Opimian wine but in the must unto them.' Sir Thomas Browne, with his pompous, rolling periods, calls up hallucinatory visions of wines that out-Methuselah Methuselah. I have heard of wine-lovers who have sought to restore the fragrance of the dried-up lees still left in an Egyptian wine-jar, buried thousands of years before the death of Homer; some, greatly daring, claim that they can recognize in the solidified wine that after eighteen centuries remained in the *amphorae* of Pompeii the distinctive flavour of the local wine. Great is the power of imagination: I might be more inclined to believe them if I had ever been able to detect anything exceptional or distinctive in the wines of the district. Pliny, at any rate, who perished on the day those wines were buried, says that the Pompeian wines were at their best at the age of ten, and gained nothing by increased age.

Today we cherish less favourable opinions of the wines of the ancients than Sir Thomas Browne, and when I was at school there was a disposition to think of all Roman wines as sticky syrups concentrated almost to the consistency of a jelly. This idea I think was mistaken; it seems to have arisen from the amount of space given to boiled-down must, the Portuguese *jeropiga*, in the practical Latin wine manuals, which are naturally more concerned with the expedients required in a bad vintage than with the relatively simple operations needed in a good year. Martial, at any rate, talks of this treacly concoction known as *defrutum* with great contempt. However, nicety of taste was not to be expected from a people so barbarously vulgar as the Romans of the Empire.

The word *chambrer* had no Latin equivalent, and they appear to have mixed their wine indiscriminately with either hot water or snow. Depressed by the sight of the Mausoleum of Augustus, which was in view of his house, Martial proposes to banish the thought of death by making merry with bumpers of Falernian, iced with the snow preserved into the summer, and then spoils any prospect of enjoying his wine by drenching his hair in perfume. And yet in one epigram he says that he prefers to smell of nothing than of scent.

It seems to have been equally correct to take your Falernian with hot water. The knights at the theatre, where they were allowed free wine, mixed it with warm water, and one epigram tells us, 'If you are drinking your wine hot, *murrha* is specially suitable for mulled Falernian and gives it a finer flavour.' It is doubtful what *murrha* really was, but it certainly provided the material from which the most fashionable and expensive drinking vessels were made. It came from the East and it has been suggested that it was porcelain, but it seems rather to have been some kind of stone or crystal. The cups made from it were thin and easily broken and of many colours, 'mottled' Martial calls them. Their value depended on the way in which they were coloured; from the description of Pliny they seem sometimes to have shown the hues of the opal and at other times to have been variegated with the colours of the rainbow. One does not see why they should have been particularly suitable for hot Falernian. The Romans had no idea of the charms lent by the transparency of fine glass to the colour of wine. We set great store on being able to contemplate its reds and purples with no opacity to interfere with the natural purity of their hue. The Romans had both glass and crystal goblets, but they did not appreciate them for their true value; indeed they prized the murrhine cups for their opacity. No Roman would have minded drinking Cognac from a teacup or Champagne from pewter. So we find Martial complaining that the host drank himself from *murrha*, and gave his guests glasses, in order that they might not see that he was serving two wines, a good *cru* for himself and something inferior for the others. If he had drunk from glass, they would have seen the difference in the colour of the wines. Glass cups are connected with Egypt and were often highly ornamented—simplicity was not a Roman virtue— but the goblets made from rock crystal seem to have been more highly prized. Martial has an epigram about them which in these days should appeal to many a wine-lover driven by force of circumstance to do his own washing-up.

> Frangere dum metuis, franges crystallina: peccant
> Securae nimium sollicitæque manus.

> You crystal break, for fear of breaking it:
> Careless and careful hands like faults commit.

In 1893, wine was less expensive than water in Champagne, and on several occasions at the beginning of this century there were such gluts of wine in the Midi that it was poured out into the streets for want of a market. Such happenings belong to another and better world than that in which we live, even though too much wine did entail riots in Narbonne. Much the same thing must have occurred in parts of Italy in Martial's day, for he recommended the purchase at Ravenna of a water reservoir rather than a vineyard.

> Lodged at Ravenna, water sells so dear,
> A cistern to a vineyard I prefer.

But the Romans had their bad, rainy vintages, and the poet draws a sad picture of the dripping vineyard beaten with continual downpours and condoles with the wine-merchant on the fate that compels him that year to sell nothing but watered wine. It would not have been much use paying a guest to whom you were offering wine of that vintage the formal compliment, 'Vinum tu facies bonum bibendo,' 'You will make the wine good by drinking it.' There was an occasion when even this mild tipple was forbidden to Martial; for we find him cursing his doctors for putting him on the water wagon and wishing his enemies the worst fate he can think of—drinking hot water. One can understand that his digestion may have been upset if he had been indulging too freely in either Falernian or Massic, both heavy wines, thickened with honey, which must have made a very sickly drink, though he assures us that it was worthy to be mixed by Ganymede.

When all is said and done, I fear that the Romans were never really oenosophists, and they went in for wine-faking on a hair-raising scale. Cato the elder, that model of respectability, unfolds at length a recipe for making Coan wine out of Italian grapes, and very nasty it must have been. In the 'sixties of the last century, Mr. Tovey visited at Cette, now Sète, in the Roman province of *Gallia Narbonensis*, the 'extensive factories of wines of all countries— Port, Sherry, Madeira, Claret, Burgundy, or any other known wines.' It is probably not an accident that Martial, eighteen hundred years earlier, singles out this very same district as the infamous centre of all Roman wine-faking. Already in those days, these vineyards must have been the main source of ordinary wines—quantity without quality—

and so provided abundance of the basic material for the production of imitation *crus*. The region was particularly notorious for the cellars in which wines were aged by heat —smoked, for some purpose concealed from the modern wine-drinker, and generally manipulated, and Pliny bears out Martial's complaints of the rascally *fumaria* of Marseilles. 'It is impossible to describe the wines grown in the Narbonne district, for they have set up regular factories, colouring them with smoke and what is worse, adulterating them with noxious herbs and drugs.'

III

The Corkscrew in the Dark Ages

*I*o, *triumphe! Dicite io Paean, et io bis, dicite, Paean!*
I fear that my readers will not join me in these classical
ululations of triumph and joy—all the more because
a suspicion lurks at the back of my mind that the hexa-
meter from Ovid's *Ars Amatoria* celebrates a not quite
proper victory. They can scarcely be expected to share my
raptures at having run to earth at long last the elusive
iron corkscrew of Sedulius Scottus. And what, they may well
ask, is this mysterious phantom corkscrew? It made its
apparition in Miss Helen Waddell's *Mediaeval Latin Lyrics*
in the guise of a translation from a poem by the Irish-Scot
Sedulius Scottus, an ecclesiastical worthy of the ninth
century A.D.

> Doth not the cork, redolent of balsam,
> Suffer the piercing of the iron corkscrew,
> Whence from the fissure floweth out a precious
> Drop of the liquor?

So Miss Waddell translated the Latin and aroused my
curiosity, since André Simon in his *Bottlescrew Days* had
meditated on the unknown genius who invented the corkscrew and concluded that its invention—or at any rate its
introduction—must date from early in the eighteenth century at the same time as corks and bins for recumbent
bottles became indispensable accessories in the cellar. The

earliest document relating to the *bottlescrew* he had been able to trace was a rare print dated 1770. It was amusing to come across a reference both to the cork and its extractor nine centuries earlier, but perhaps not really surprising; for corks and glass bottles were unquestionably known to the Romans, and the legend about Dom Perignon and the discovery of the cork, which made the maturing of wine in general, and the making of sparkling wine in particular, possible, represents the re-discovery of a system forgotten with the downfall of Roman civilization.

It was natural that I should want to see the Latin original of Miss Waddell's translation. As luck would have it, she gave most conscientiously references to volume and page of the *Poetae Latini Carolini Aevi*, the distinctly barbarous poets of the age of Charlemagne and his successors, in the case of a number of quotations which had no particular interest for me, but she gave no hint as to where that iron corkscrew might be lurking. However, such works of Sedulius as might have been preserved were not, I thought, likely to be voluminous, and with a light heart I set out to explore a department of literature known to me only through Miss Waddell's work.

Foolishly I failed to take into account 'the total depravity of inanimate things'; indeed I hardly realized that books were both inanimate and perverse. It seemed so easy to ask the London Library for those Carolingian poets and run lightly through even such a formidable folio volume as those usually dedicated to the works of Churchmen of the Middle Ages. The devil of contradictoriness, the imp of perversity, as the librarian called him, then got to work to defeat my efforts. First the book I wanted was thought to be out, then it was found to have disappeared, and only after many weeks of search was it caught, after wandering of its own volition to a shelf where it had no right of presence whatever. Then I started on my voyage of discovery through its eight hundred pages, and the very last page to which I chanced to turn rewarded my perseverance. On it I found at last:

> Balsami cortex redolens aroma
> Ungulis ferri patiturne vulnus,
> Unde fissuris pretiosa manat
> Gutta liquoris?

'Does not the cork redolent of the aroma of balsam suffer a wound from the claws of iron, and thence through the fissures oozes a precious drop of liquor?' Miss Waddell's translation is as faithful as faithful can be. I must admit that I find the point of Sedulius' remark rather obscure; it is the last verse of a poem in Sapphic verse glorifying the military prowess of Count Eberhard of Friuli, who has been winning victories against the Saracens. It winds up with a suggestion that he should look benignly on 'the poor learned poet of Christ,' who has written him such an original and tuneful song, which presumably is to act as the corkscrew and extract a drop or two of charity from the Count's bottled up beneficence.

Ungulae ferri scarcely sound as if the cork was driven home, indeed the phrase almost smacks of the drawing of a bung from a barrel. *Ungula* has *hoof* as its first significance, but here it must be referred to the secondary meaning of *claws* or a bird's *talons*, to say nothing of an iron instrument of torture imitating them and used to tear the flesh off a prisoner's ribs. Probably we should describe the instrument as pincers such as might grasp the projecting end of a cork or bung which had not been driven home. Sedulius' simile does not persuade one that it did its work very well. When one draws a cork, it is not satisfactory for it to break so that the wine oozes through its fissures, and one may observe that it is *fissures* and not *fissure*, so that we must conceive the cork splitting or crumbling all to pieces as it does with a thoroughly bad corkscrew.

Once again I raise a lamentation which is always in season over the presumptuous inefficiency of the average corkscrew-maker. Most of them seem to know of no stoppers of bottles other than the hard corks of ginger pop and the like which surrender to the rounded spiral of the gimblet. It is comparatively rare to find the corkscrew with flattened thread which, unlike the gimlet, will not tear out the heart of an ancient cork. And even then it is probably too short, by its failure to transfix from top to bottom leaving in the neck a maddening slice of cork, which will probably be pushed into the bottle. I have spoken of the total depravity of inanimate objects; no unliving thing is more depraved than the corkscrew genus. A well-known firm, many years ago, determined to encourage the wine-lover and prove that the extraction of a cork is the merest child's play, presented their customers with ideal corkscrews by the hundred. One of those corkscrews was given to me and I carried it home rejoicing, confident that it would make the tolerable corkscrew already in my possession look very small. In appearance it was perfect, thread beautifully flattened and length sufficient to transfix the longest cork and to spare, but could I persuade it to bore its way down the centre of the cork? No. This feat afforded no difficulty to my other modest corkscrews, but I was absolutely defeated in all my efforts by the ideal corkscrew. It seemed to have but one purpose, to screw itself out through the neck of the bottle. Convinced that I must be at fault, I took that corkscrew to my good friend Walter Berry and invited him to put it to its proper use. With a hint of supercilious eyebrows at my amateurish clumsiness, he began to show me how to drive a corkscrew down the centre of a cork. Two turns, three turns—he stopped and frowned . . . reversed the motion and unscrewed, tried again, again a retreat. Then looking at the bottlescrew against the light, we discerned the trick of its depravity. At first sight, it appeared perfectly symmetrical, but closer inspection showed that the line of its spiral with the handle was just enough out of the true to make it quite impossible to transfix a cork with it. I have often wondered how many good

61

people were reduced to despair by that almost unnoticeable trick of bad fashioning.

But I must go back to Sedulius, for even apart from his corkscrew he deserves attention as a wine-lover who like us was well acquainted with the pangs of austerity. Though he lived a thousand years ago, he liked wine as well as the best Irishman—Maurice Healy perhaps—of our own time. With two other Irishmen, he migrated to Liége, where he was welcomed by the bishop as a scholar. Never in his pious hymns or in his duteous exaltations of Kings, Bishops and other dignitaries, did he show the slightest scruple about manifesting his great thirst—not for beer, the horrible Liége Beer, but for the 'dewy gifts of Bacchus,' the good Rhine wine, which inspired his *saturated*, his *well-soaked*, poems.

Poor old Sedulius lived in a barbarous war-torn age with civilization in its infancy, or rather paralysed and dying after the fall of the Roman Empire. Charlemagne and his Franks were a long way from replacing the wisdom and arts of Greece and the luxury of Rome. Our friend is so pleasantly shameless in his begging, when he sends a spring poem to his Bishop. His livelihood depended on his learning—men were simple enough in those days to set great store by the wisdom and knowledge they themselves did not possess— and he worked hard in his Dog Latin to persuade his patrons that he deserved all the good things he so much liked, particularly wine. Once he was stranded without Bacchus, mead or even beer, when all the countryside was gay with spring, and he cries to the Bishop that he is his lordship's Orpheus and the ox that treads out the corn worthy of his hire. To Count Robert he sends some 'rhythmical versicles,' which seem to refer to him a gift of twenty-five dozen flagons of Rhenish wine. As Miss Waddell says, they still read a little drunk with their combination of thirst and piety. Moselle and Rhenish and a thousand barrels full of fine wine thunder out the Count's praises, and since he has bestowed largesse of Falernian on the humble and meek, in other words Sedulius, the Saints will see that he is well provided with abundant draughts from the fountain of eternal life. Less grateful were the streams of Siloam than the Count's gifts of wine. 'I sucked them up,' cries Sedulius, 'I do not deny it; what's more I'll suck them up again—a long farewell to swipes!'

There is often a touch of the brogue in Sedulius' elegiacs and we find him writing a kind of Quaker's Chorus for the brethren on the feast of Saint Vedastus, whoever that holy man may be. It opens with an appeal to Bacchus asking for the kisses of peace that only the wine-cup can give. Then there is a pun about Bacchus under the name of Liber and *liber* meaning *free*. A prayer probably highly appropriate to the occasion is raised to the holy Vedastus that the brethren may not be knocked out by the strength of their potations, but may enjoy them fully and have their hearts made glad. Puns follow about measures of wine and measures of moderation with six pints to a man and six men to the six feet of the Latin iambic for 'The more we drink together, the merrier we shall be.'

The tragedy of the exiled Irishmen reaches its height when in their Bishop's absence they are oppressed not only by thirst but also by hunger. They have neither wines nor mead and bread is short, and there is just the horrible Liége swipes which is making the wise men lean. No grain went to its brewing; it is just undrinkable, banishing cheerfulness and bringing sadness. It owes nothing to the Jordan or the river which is the daughter of Moses—the Moselle thus taken in kinship with Moses as if it were a tributary of the Nile provides an agreeable surprise—but it is the produce of that muddiest of streams, the brook Cedron. It has stolen the colour of the grain, but not a morsel of grain is in its composition. Call it rather a wild beast fit only for the rivers of Hell and it has worked such havoc with Sedulius' inside that he implores the lord Bishop to

63

send him a poultice at once. The Bishop, we understand from a postscript, read Sedulius' complaint and chuckled, and sent the poet that Bacchic poultice for which he prayed.

It is curious how strongly these Irish scholars of the ninth century living in the north of Europe, whose only acquaintance with vineyards was likely to have been gathered in the course of a pilgrimage to Rome, clamour for wine and despise beer as of nothing worth. It is true that Alcuin, summoned by Charlemagne from York in order that both he and his empire might go to school, was not an Irishman but a Yorkshireman; it is he who opens the chorus of lamentation, when his friends had run out of wine and bitter beer raged in their bellies. He loved the nightingale and the cuckoo, and was mightily afraid that the cuckoo might be drowned in his flight across the seas and spring never come again, and it was his joy to be able to send the Archbishop presents of wine from the Continent as well as books for his library.

It was an Irishman later who bewailed his fate since all his learning earned him nothing except a little very bad bread and a few drops of abominable beer. Yet another of these Irish Scots who lived at Soissons shoots an epigram winged with scorn at *cervisa*, the word for beer still preserved in the Spanish *cerveza*, 'Off you go, beer! Bacchus, I summon you by your ancient pagan name, come and swamp beer with wine.'

Doubtless the beer of those days was thoroughly unpalatable to those who were not broken to the sourness and windy weakness of badly brewed ale. The Romans first came across malted liquor in Gaul, and Virgil apparently refers to it in the Third Georgic as the drink of the Scythians, who represented for his contemporary the inhabitants of the polar regions as the Esquimaux do for us. The poet says that they wear skins, live in caves and make the night merry with potations that imitate the juice of the grape *fermento atque acidis sorbis.* Some commentators take the Latin to mean beer and cider, *fermentum* being the fermentation of barley, wheat or oats, and the *sorbi* being cider apples or any other kind of sour fruit that can be converted into alcoholic liquor. Certainly *fermentum* meant yeast for Pliny, and both cider and perry were known to Palladius, a versifying farmer of the fourth century A.D., who talks of making wine from apples in October and from the strained juice of pressed pears. It is safe to bet that in Roman times all these drinks were much better made than they were after the barbarian invasions, and wine must have owed its pre-eminence to the fact that quite palatable beverage could be produced from fermented grape-juice almost by rule of thumb.

After studying the conditions in which our countrymen exchange their learning for wines that made glad their hearts a thousand years ago, we may find some trifle of consolation for our own evil fate, banished in a way those forbears could never have understood from the sun and the vine. There was no one to forbid them to take any money they might possess and to spend all the time they liked in a Europe, which might be difficult and dangerous for the traveller, but which was not partitioned with passport and customs regulations and impenetrable Iron Curtains.

IV

Good Fellowship in Chaucer's England

T HE *Canterbury Tales* is the wine-lover's bedside book. Chaucer, the son of a vintner in Upper Thames Street, had learnt as a boy all that was to be learnt about wine in England, and in later life as an Ambassador gained familiarity with the finest wines of many lands. This knowledge of his is continually flashing up in his verse, and no excuse is needed for any student of wine who turns to his poems for instruction in the history of the Art of Good Living. His age was an age of good fellowship. The motley company that set out from the 'Tabard' at Southwark on its pilgrimage to St. Thomas à Becket's tomb, at the most lovely moment of spring, included all classes of society from the poet, a man of the world who stood high in the King's councils, and the Knight who had served with great distinction all over the world, clerics of varying importance, the Prioress, representatives of the well-to-do middle classes, down to such humble folk as the carpenter, weaver, ploughman and so on. They rode their way and told their stories all on an equal footing, and Harry Bailey, the host of the 'Tabard' and master of the ceremonies, made no more bones about stinting Chaucer of his tale of Sir Thopas and cutting him short than he did of telling the miller he was drunk or the monk that his tragic stories of fallen greatness were not

66

worth a butterfly. Just as they accepted their class distinctions without vulgarity or snobbery, so they seem to have shared one another's liking both for wine and beer, taking gratefully whichever came handiest to the mouth. How ridiculous it is to talk of progress, when one thinks that in those happy days wine was nearly as cheap and plentiful in this non-wine-growing country as it was in France! So marvellously have we speeded up communications and, as we are continually boasting, made the world smaller, that wine has become a fabulous luxury and that a man would be thought mad if he asked at a wayside inn for a pint of Claret.

If folk went on pilgrimage in these days, they would go by motor-coach and precious little good fellowship would there be in their journey. Fixed hasty stoppages after passing through an unseen countryside would give occasion to swallow some watery beer; none of that 'moyst corny ale,' 'fresh strong ale,' that ale of Southwark, which almost prevented the Miller from sitting his horse, though it did not prevent him telling his rude story. What hope would there be of anybody in a motor-coach telling his fellow companions a story whether polite or impolite? I remember how before the last war Walter Berry took a whole coach load of Knights of the Round Table on pilgrimage to Glastonbury to do reverence to I know not what supposed relic of King Arthur, and though we were a very jolly party and honoured the god of wine with a devotion worthy of Chaucer's pilgrims, there was no possibility of story-telling and very little of private conversation, while the char-à-banc de luxe pursued its headlong career. As for the countryside through which we passed, we caught passing glimpses of it, but we may have passed through a score of villages with names as delightful as Chaucer's 'litel toun which that y'cleped is Bob-up-and-down' and never known it.

No doubt we were more lazily luxurious conveyed by petrol and machinery than those earlier pilgrims jogging along on their horses, but how much we missed by saving

time and trouble! We spent the night at Bath, and I am
sure Walter would, if it had been suggested, have recreated
the Chaucerian atmosphere by giving us the Franklin's
favourite breakfast, offering us the sop in wine of which
that epicure in whose house it snowed of meat and drink,
of all dainties that men could think, was so fond in the
early morning, though perhaps we should have had difficulty
in deciding in what wine the sop of bread was to be soaked.
Certainly, though our host had seen to it that wonderful
meals awaited us everywhere, we had no cook such as
Chaucer had 'to boil the chickens with the marrow-bones,'
to say nothing of making poudre-marchant tart and galin-
gale, spices from the East to which our ancestors were so
partial, roasting, seething, broiling, frying, baking pies,
thickening soups, and his chef d'œuvre *blankmanger*, a dish
which I felt sure must be that blanc-mange which I have
detested since my childhood; but the learned Skeat suggests
a more palatable compound made of minced capon with
cream, sugar and flour. *Pace* his scholarship, I do not feel
quite sure about the sugar; it does not seem to go very well
with the chicken, and though it is mentioned in Chaucer as
the component of a sweetmeat it was a rarity and luxury,
honey being the accepted sweetener. Not having Chaucer's
cook, we were saved the embarrassment of putting him
back in the saddle after he had fallen off his horse owing to
an excessive affection for London ale. 'There was great
shoving both to and fro, To lifte him up, and muchel care
and woe.' Yet after he had been remounted, he swigged
'a draught of wine of a ripe grape,' and therefore presumably strong and good, offered him by the Manciple,
and does not seem to have again lost his equilibrium.

Though on our Glastonbury jaunt we had a wine-shipper
in the party, we had no representative of the sea such as
Chaucer's Shipman, the master of the barge *Maudelayne*,
who made his foes walk the plank and many times and oft
drew a draught of wine from the casks of Bordeaux wine

in his cargo, while the trader who was importing them to England was asleep. We may imagine accordingly that he knew what he was talking about when he told in his tale how the Monk, who had an eye to the wife of his friend, the Merchant of St. Denis, made himself a welcome guest by bringing with him on his visit a *jubbe of Malvesye*, and eek another full of fine Vernage, and *volatyl*, otherwise fowls. There is something I find soul-satisfying about the word *jubbe*, both in its sound and its capacity; I guess that it was an earthenware jar and know from the authority already quoted that it held four gallons; one might certainly hope to win a smile if nothing more bringing as part of one's rations the equivalent of four dozen bottles of wines highly esteemed by the taste of the time. Simon says in his *Encyclopaedia* that Malvoisie from Cyprus and Vernage from Florence were dessert wines, not for the thirsty, but to be sipped and enjoyed when friend met friend for pleasure's sake or hospitality, so that the allowance of a *jubbe* of each was a generous one, especially as the Merchant went off to Bruges on his business on the third day. Malvoisie or Malmsey of Madeira remains among my memories of really great wines, and Malmsey of Cyprus, remarkable for great age and a strong taste of cedar pencil, I have tasted, but the Malmsey of Candia in Crete, once a valuable Venetian cargo, disappeared centuries ago. Vernage, Italian *vernaccia*, is the name of a grape grown in many parts of Italy and producing a sweet white wine. It may have been shipped by the wine-merchants of Florence to this country, but I do not think that it was ever grown in the Chianti country. More probably it came from Verona where to this day they produce an agreeable sweetish white wine of good repute under the name of Soave. One last word as to the *jubbe*—it was with a *jubbe* of good ale with bread and cheese 'sufficing right enough as for a day,' that the silly carpenter victualled the kneading trough and the two tubs, which were to serve as arks for himself, Alison his pretty

69

wife, and Nicholas the naughty clerk, when the second flood came; four gallons of ale for each of them would seem generous provision.

Chaucer was in burlesque vein when he rhymed the Tale of Sir Thopas, which brought down on his head the wrath of Harry Bailey—rhyme doggerel, said mine host, that made his ears ache. In this spirit, the poet sets out the training diet on which the knight 'fair and gent' prepared to fight a giant with three heads 'for paramour and jolitee.' First his merry men brought him sweet wine, and also mead in a mazer; we are not told whether he drank them together or alternately, but the combination sounds a trifle indigestible for a man who is going to fight for his life. We are told that these beverages were to wash down a royal spice mixture of gingerbread, liquorice and cummin with some of the best sugar. The effect of this meal taken while he was being armed was perhaps best shown by what he did when he rode forth to look for his enemy: 'Himself drank water of the well, As did the knight Sir Percival.' The Doctor of Physic who was also of the company would scarcely have approved such training fare; for we are told that of his diet measurable was he, for it was of no superfluity, but of great nourishing and digestible.

The Somnour, who summoned delinquents before the ecclesiastical courts and whose mildest vice was blackmail, would have been wise to consult the Doctor; for his face as fiery red as a cherub's was a mass of pimples, whelkes and knobs sitting on his cheeks, like Bardolph's face, 'all bubukles and whelks, and knobs, and flames o' fire,' and no ointment would do anything for his complexion. Well loved he garlic, onions, to say nothing of leeks, and to drink strong wine red as blood. When he had drunk enough wine, he would speak nothing but Latin of which he knew a few legal terms which he had picked up in court without knowing what they meant. His English, however, in the unpleasantly coarse tale against Friars which was his con-

70

tribution to the party's entertainment, is garnished with some most expressive words and phrases. How better could one describe the son of Belial flushed with insolence and wine than *all vinolent as bottle in the spence, as full of wine as a bottle in the buttery,* fat as a whale, and walking as a swan. *Dronkelewe* is a pleasant term for *addicted to drink,* especially when applied to irous Cambyses, and there is something picturesque in *angry as a pissemire,* though it seems rather unjust to take the pismire or ant as a symbol of bad temper.

Perhaps the greatest joy in reading the *Canterbury Tales* is this discovery of words full of vivid imagery with their meaning still bright and unclipped by over-use. Nowadays we cross the Atlantic for the enrichment of our language with the impressionist slang, which pushes aside the verbal currency that has lost the sharpness of outline it once had and has degenerated into the worn flatness of the *cliché.* It would be so easy to turn to the first of supreme English poets and glean from him a wealth of expressions which by their aptness and realism reduce the most brilliantly acrobatic American slang to the commonplace and dull vulgarity. I am not sure whether *a-blake-beried* in the Pardoner's sense of 'a-blackberrying, i.e. a-wandering at will, astray'—I quote Skeat's vocabulary—refers to the gathering of the wild fruit or the bramble's helter-skelter way of growing, but I am certain it is an expressive way of referring to souls who after death arrive at the wrong destination. It would be nice when one offers a friend a chicken to call it *volatyl* like the Merchant's Monk, and going 'upon the viritoot' is more pleasing to the ear than the razzle-dazzle or the bust, while the lady who was *somdel smoterlich* and full of *hoker and bisemare* is onomatopœically described as smirched in reputation and full of haughtiness and pride. I have no idea why *thedom* should mean *success,* though the reason might stare me in the face with a slight change in spelling, but *swink* for *toil, wlatsom* for *disgusting, quad* for *evil* and so on explain themselves, and it is a pity they have become obsolete. In the Monk's tale of tragedies we learn that Samson never drank *sicer* nor wine, and *sicer* according to the vocabulary means *strong drink*. It is a Greek word used in the Septuagint translation of the Old Testament for any intoxicating liquor other than wine, so that it covers beer, cider and all home-made wines such as cowslip, elderberry and the like, though I have no reason to suppose that the ancient Hebrews knew anything of cowslips or elderberries or their vinous possibilities.

I have mentioned the Shipman, a reckless fellow of no tender conscience, who used to steal the wine he was bringing from Bordeaux, while the Merchant was asleep. It was a trick as old as ships and wine, and to this day a wealth of ingenuity is expended on the illegitimate tapping of wine and spirit casks on long voyages. The journey down the Douro from the Quintas to Oporto cannot be described as long, but in the days when the wine was brought downstream by boat, the boatmen made a habit of drinking their fill from their cargo and making up the deficiency with river water. This unfortunate failing eventually did them out of their job and made the world poorer through the substitution of the motor lorry for the picturesque craft that used to carry out this traffic.

It is in connection with the Pardoner, the dealer in sham relics fresh from Rome, and his tale that Chaucer gives the clearest evidence of his close acquaintance with wine-merchants and their ways. The Pardoner was an effeminate fellow with a voice like a goat and long yellow locks falling over his shoulders, but he liked good cheer. Harry Bailey called upon him to entertain the company with a tale of mirth and japes, complaining that the sad story of Virginia just told by the Doctor of Physic had so distressed him as almost to give him heart disease. The only things that could put him right were either a *triacle*, a sovereign remedy, says the Glossary—how melancholy a degradation for a sovereign panacea to come down to the tank of *treacle*—or else a draught of *moyst* and *corny* ale such as he would no doubt have swallowed, if he had still been at the 'Tabard,' or the immediate telling of a merry tale. *Corny* implies that the ale was 'strong of the corn or malt' according to Skeat. *Moyst* means fresh, he adds, but he does not tell us why. On the face of it there is no reason why fresh ale should be any moister than old, since they are both equally liquid. The *Concise Oxford Dictionary* is no help, since it is content to derive the word from Old French *moiste* of doubtful origin. Another dictionary, however, comes to the rescue, ascribing to *moiste* an illuminating derivation from *mustus, new and juicy*, whence *mustum* the new fermenting wine, so that moist or moisty ale is directly related to the must that foams in the wine press. Sir Thopas, it may be added, rode through a forest in which there grew a number of odd herbs, liquorice, setwall or zedoary, a kind of valerian, cloves, and 'notemuge to put in ale whether it be moyst or stale.' We are left to guess how the Knight who was born at Poperinghe found himself in the Spice Islands, where all the birds in the forest were English, but his nutmeg was presumably for spiced ale and the meaning of *moyst* is illustrated by its opposition to *stale*. Old ale, of course, was not necessarily stale. The Manciple, after they had got the drunken Cook back on his horse, says that the fellow would tell his tale badly: for were it wine, or old or moisty ale that he had drunk, he 'speketh in his nose, and fneseth fast, and eek he hath the pose,' in other words, he talked through his nose like the Elephant's child when the Crocodile was pulling his nose out into a trunk, puffed and blew after the fashion suggested by the sound of *fneseth*, and really seemed to have a cold in the head. *Pose* looks an unlikely word for a cold in the head, and perhaps it applies specially to a drunken catarrh. The Reve or Bailiff describes the condition of the Miller after he had drink taken and 'varnished' his head: 'He yexeth, and he speketh through the nose, as

73

he were on the quack, or on the pose'; *yexing* stands for the hiccoughs and he was as hoarse as a quacking duck to say nothing of a cold in the head.

To return to our Pardoner, he thought over what he was going to say, while he took a drink of corny ale and ate a cake at an alestake, that is the pole sticking out from an ale-house to carry the pole or bush, the part being put for the whole. He enjoyed his beer, though he confessed that he liked drinking the liquor of the vine as well as having a wench in every town. None the less he opened his tale with an eloquent tirade against gluttony and drunkenness, and in the course of it Chaucer wrote the lines that have become a *locus classicus* concerning the fourteenth-century wine trade.

> Now keep ye from the white and from the red,
> And namely from the white wine of Lepe,
> That is to sell in Fish Street or in Chepe.
> This wine of Spain creepeth subtilly
> In other wines, growing fast by,
> Of which there riseth such fumositee,
> That when a man hath drunken draughtes three,
> And weneth that he be at home in Chepe,
> He is in Spain, right at the town of Lepe,
> Not at the Rochelle, nor at Bordeaux town.

Under the heading 'Chaucer,' Simon's *Encyclopaedia* tells us that Lepe is now Niebla between Seville and Moguer and classes it with the expensive dessert wines Malmsey and Vernage. Lepe is in the same province, the Province of Huelva, as Niebla, but it is some seventy kilometers away from that town, and I cannot believe that it was an expensive wine; for expensive wines are not used for the sophistication of beverage wines. Lepe was evidently sold under its own name in the City of London near Chaucer's home, and was also used for the fraudulent adulteration of the French wines from Bordeaux and La Rochelle. Its *fumosity*—delightful word!—found its way into the weaker French wines with the result that three glasses would go to a man's head. Then he would be transported neither to La Rochelle nor Bordeaux, where the fumes of his wine would have taken him, if they had spirited him off to their supposed place of origin, but to Lepe, the home of the strong wine predominant in the mixture.

English wine-drinkers were always complaining about the way the inn-keepers adulterated their wines by fraudulent mixtures—*Pasquil's Palimodia* (1609) tells of *close-cellar jumblings* and resulting *false impostured wines*— and the law prescribed that only certain wines might be stored together in the same cellar. Sr. D. Manuel González of González Byass tells me that the Lepe wines are white, dry and not particularly strong and thinks that they have always been so. He believes that the Chaucer reference can only mean that the Lepe wines were already being fortified, as undoubtedly Sack was, at a later period, and in that case we have in this passage the earliest mention of a fortified wine so far recorded. The wines of the Douro were not fortified until the eighteenth century. Thanks to the Moors, the Spaniards were the first European nation to know about distillation, and I am convinced that the popularity of Spanish wines in this country was largely due to the added alcohol, which not only removed them from the category of Falstaff's *thin potations*, but enabled them to age. Sack prided itself on being old, when old French wines were sold off cheap.

75

V

Sparkle and Bubble in the Poets

JOHN GAY, best known to us as the author of the *Beggar's Opera*, devoted his earliest poem to the subject of *Wine*. In was written in 1708, when he was twenty, and Professor Saintsbury describes it as 'clever enough Miltonic parody' in a sentence that set me looking it up. It cannot be described as exactly inspiring to the lover of poetry; the parody of *Paradise Lost* is a bit too obvious and facile and it is too easy to guess what the writer.is going to say before one reads him. It does, however, possess a minor interest for the wine-lover, who cares to study the history of the art of wine-drinking.

> Of Happiness Terrestrial, and the Source.
> Whence human pleasures flow, sing Heavenly Muse,

was an almost inevitable opening, though one may welcome such a line as 'Thy charming sight, but much more charming Gust' in which the Latin *gustus* is faithfully preserved. The British mariner, it seems, went to sea to pay Wine homage and receive its blessings, and Gay paints us a pleasant picture of the sea-salt gazing with delight on the 'purple Grape in largest Clusters Pendant,'

> Whether at Lusitanian sultry coasts,
> Or lofty Teneriff, Palma, Ferro,
> Provence, Or at the Celtiberian Shores.

76

After a glance at Horace for whom

> Choicest Nectarian juice Crown'd largest Bowles,
> And Overlook'd the lid, alluring sight,
> Of fragrant Scent attractive, tast Divine,

we pass to what appears to be a City wine-shop in the days of Queen Anne, up a flight of stairs. At the top a Majestic Dame, enclosed in a semicircular throne, deals with the orders, as the waiters bawl out words unintelligible, and knowing 'the Jargon Sound' writes out 'in characters mysterious words obscure.'

The Head Waiter asks the customers what they will have to drink in the following 'Florid Speech'.

> Name, Sirs, the WINE that most invites your Tast.
> Champaign or Burgundy, or Florence pure,
> Or Hock Antique, or Lisbon New or Old,
> Bordeaux, or neat French white, or Alicant.

Gay's party declare for Bordeaux with 'voice unanimous,' and the waiter goes off to return with a bottle in one hand, and in the other capacious, glistering glasses. The bottle is full fraught with goodly wine, which we presume was drawn from the wood to judge from the reckless way in which it was poured; it sounds almost as if the waiter wanted to put a head on the Claret.

> He with extended Hand,
> Rais'd high, pours forth the Sanguin frothy Juice,
> O'erspread with Bubbles, dissipated soon.

After the filling of the glasses, they turn to drinking toasts to the Queen, first clinking glasses, and then to anybody else they might think of until

> All Blithe and Jolly that like Arthur's Knights,
> Of Rotund Table, Fam'd in Pristin Records,
> Now most we seem'd; such is the Power of Wine.

Alas! that I cannot draw the attention of the late Charles Walter Berry to the last three lines. That eminent wine-lover and Remembrancer of the Knights of the Round Table would have found in them a source of unending pleasure and inspiration. Gay enlarges on sparkling juices and frothy sprightly wine as though he and his friends liked their wines well shaken up; in all probability the Champagne offered by the waiter was still.

A hundred years later, we find Keats haunted by this rather curious notion of the sparkle of a still red wine; for I am sure that none of us who enjoy his poetry will admit that there can be any glorification in his verse of the unnatural perversity of sparkling Burgundy. No doubt his mind was on wine in the wood when he wrote

> the splendour of the revelries,
> When butts of wine are drunk off to the lees.

A bit barbarous that age of chivalry one fears, when the tournament, or whatever the entertainment might be, called for jollity on lees and sediment.

There seems a touch of Gay's wine waiter pouring out Bordeaux in that trance when the poet

> sees white coursers paw and prance,
> Bestridden of gay knights, in gay apparel,
> Who at each other tilt in playful quarrel . . .
> And, when upheld, the wine from each bright jar
> Pours with the lustre of a falling star.

There must have been a wide gap with many a chance for a slip between the glass and the decanter.

> Hast thou a goblet for dark sparkling wine?
> That goblet right heavy, and massy, and gold?

The answer is in the negative, if the poet is really thinking of some gaudy champagnized beverage.

Again in *Endymion* there is a wine 'alive with sparkles, never, I aver, so cool a purple,' and Ganymede is given a

78

strange and seemingly contradictory instruction, when he is told to

> Let the red wine within the goblet boil
> Cold as a bubbling well.

Are we to take it that this still red wine with its sparkle is imperfectly fermented, and that this particular attraction is to be classified with that hint of effervescence, which I must admit delights me in a young Moselle. It is very wrong to enjoy a wine that has not been fully fermented, and I can only defend my bad taste with the excuse of extreme youth that many many years ago I was mightily refreshed in Italy by a Barbaresco, a red wine that had more than a hint of sparkle, which can only have been due to imperfect fermentation. There is more than a touch of asperity in Ian Campbell's criticism of certain young Moselles. 'I confess the prickle of fermentation in some (cleverly *admired* as *spritzig* by the Germans) does not appeal to me.' There is no doubt about it; the purist in wine doctrines must look askance on that juice of the grape in which the miracle of Cana in Galilee has not been carried through to its final consummation. Yet how attractive was the stimulating tingle on the tongue of the light wines drunk in that country, where no man goes out for a walk without a corkscrew in his pocket! I refer to the vineyards of the Moselle. And indeed such a connoisseur as Rudd did not turn up his nose at wines that had just a trace of splutter such as the god of still wines frown upon. In *Hocks and Moselles*, he writes of that sparkle or *spritz* that is so attractive in Moselle wines. 'Very delightful it is, too: as long as it is only just a prickle.' Few wines can have given Walter Berry towards the end of his life so much pleasure as Moselle, and I never remember him making any complaint about the *spritz*.

Keats was certainly alive to the fascination of wine, but I fear that he was more familiar with it in literature than

79

in the glass and sometimes he seems to treat the fermented juice of the grape in a very odd way.

> For as delicious wine, doth, sparkling, dive
> In nectar'd clouds and curls through water fair,
> So from the arbour roof down swell'd an air
> Odorous and enlivening.

This dropping of drops of wines however delicious into water however pure appears to be more than a little wasteful, and I should like to think that Keats was really thinking of absinthe curdling into opalescence, though in that case it would be drops of water that were falling into the glass.

For Keats the wine must sparkle even when it is being poured into water, and what he meant is explained once and for all in one of the most divine poems that ever poet penned, making all criticism captious and cavilling contemptible.

> O, for a draught of vintage! that hath been
> Cool'd a long age in the deep-delvèd earth,
> Tasting of Flora and the country green,
> Dance, and Provençal song, and sunburnt mirth!
> O for a beaker full of the warm South,
> Full of the true, the blushful Hippocrene,
> With beaded bubbles winking at the brim,
> And purple-stained mouth!

In these perfect lines we can see what Keats was aiming at in all those other wine references on which we have animadverted perhaps a trifle unkindly. He is dreaming of a hot day in a sunny climate, and a draught of heady, yet cool and refreshing, Rhône wine, with a sparkle not of effervescence but of rubies, and a rich purple hue too young to have attained the onion-peel tinge of old age. For it is part of the picture that the wine should have in it a tang of the earth and a taste of flowers that the fanciful may detect in Tuscan Montepulciano. Once indeed in Italy, though in Sicily and not in Tuscany, I lighted on that beaker of the blushful Hippocrene. Above Taormina, there is a precipitous

80

crag called Mola and thither one blazing day in spring I toiled up a break-neck path to the ruins of a castle looking out over the terrible beauty of Etna, the god of fire and lava. I had little hope of refreshment, until I returned to my starting-point, but on the very peak I found a rustic table with some crazy chairs, and a peasant woman waiting to offer hospitality. There was a tiny one-roomed cottage built of stones filched from the fortress, and below it was scooped out deep underground a small cellar holding three or four barrels in an atmosphere of pleasant freshness redolent of sweet fresh earth and the scent of wine. Very cool and ruby-bright was the wine that she drew and brought up into the hot sun above, and as our thirst revelled in the chilly stimulus of its earthy tang, she told us that we were drinking the wine of Monte Venere, and it did not take much classical learning to conclude that it came from a vineyard that had once surrounded a temple of Venus just as the vineyards that once gave the name to Liebfraumilch are gathered round the Liebfrauenkirche of Worms. Our hostess led us to the castle parapet to see far below the Venus vineyards where the grapes from which our wine had been pressed had grown and there were traces of ancient ruins among the vine-stocks. With pride she sang the praises of her vineyard, its superiority over all its neighbouring rivals, its exceptional exposure and position, and the incomparable merits of its wine.

All this journey through the world of poetry has raised a problem, which needs a moment's thought. The application of the word *sparkle* to a wine that definitely claims the stillness of deep waters may be seriously justified by the lively brightness of its colour, but what about the temperature that the poet continually harps on as perfection? The red wines of Helicon appear always to be drunk, not indeed iced, but exceedingly cold. Many people seem to apply to all red wines the rule of Claret, which is at its best at the temperature of the room in which it is drunk, though on

81　　　　　　　　　　　　　　　F

no account should it be raised to that temperature by artificial and violent means. Actually, however, I think the red wines of the Rhône, Hermitage and Châteauneuf du Pape should be drunk at a lower temperature, cold enough to produce on the palate an invigorating sense of freshness. Their qualities are not qualities of delicacy, which are obscured by any intrusion of heat or cold; rather their vigour and tendency to coarseness is mitigated by a slight numbing of the faculty of taste.

Most wine-lovers are agreed that Burgundy should be drunk at a lower temperature than Claret, and Marcel Boulestin in his restaurant instructed his waiters to serve all Burgundy at cellar temperature whether the customer liked it or not. There is a good deal to be said for Professor Mathieu's theory that a wine with a high alcoholic content should be drunk colder than one with low, though all white wines call out for cold. The Bordeaux wine expert argued that cold diminishes the sensibility of the palate to the sensations exclusively due to the presence of alcohol and so brings out the non-alcoholic constituents of the wine. Ian Campbell has always insisted on the value of a low temperature in toning down excessive sweetness in a wine and once remarked to me, though I do not think he refers to the question in *Wayward Tendrils of the Vine*, that sweet Champagne and Sauternes, which are apt to cloy the average English palate, lose their extravagance of sweetness when drunk extremely cold.

VI

Wine in the Eighteenth Century with Special Reference to Port

THERE are plenty of references to wine in that voluminous eighteenth-century correspondence which has preserved for us so vivid a picture of the customs and manners of our ancestors. It was not a time of delicacy or refinement, and though they were very fond of wine, often disastrously so, they were far more concerned with quantity than quality, and I fear that the fashionable Wit, Macaroni, and Dandy—one succeeded the other chronologically—took more interest in the *kick* or intoxicating capacity of the wine which he drank with mind fixed on the vicissitudes of the gambling table, rather than in its more subtle and artistic qualities. It is unlikely that Mr. Thomas Scrope, who writes to tell the enigmatic Prince of the Wits, George Augustus Selwyn, of the disastrous results of being made 'mad' by *drinking four bottles*, either knew or cared about the quality of the wine they had contained. He terrified into hysterics a gathering of ladies of the highest society met at Tunbridge Wells including that famous, not to say notorious, beauty Miss Chudleigh, who as Duchess of Kingston was tried by the House of Lords for bigamy and who cultivated fits as part of her charm, by shooting into their midst out of a sedan chair what seemed to be a dead man, though he was only dead to the world in the alcoholic sense.

Selwyn himself was a very odd person, whom we mainly see through his reflections in the minds of his correspondents, for hardly anything he wrote has survived and most of the epigrams which made him famous and the Arbiter of Elegance have worn very thin with time and change of fashion. He was devoted to children and at the same time cherished a passion for the macabre. No execution was complete without his presence, and corpses and coffins were his heart's delight. He also cherished a taste for red wine, and though one of his friends, the Earl of Carlisle, tells him he is no judge of Claret, he seems to have had a good palate for Burgundy. As he was a friend of Horace Walpole's and one of the Advisory Committee of the Strawberry Villa, he should have taken interest in connoisseurship, though 'Horry' himself was too afraid of the gout to be a wine man.

When Selwyn was in Paris, Gilly Williams, another Wit and member of the Advisory Committee that Walpole called his *partie quarrée* or *out of town party*, wrote to him from Matson, Selwyn's family mansion, near Gloucester,

I will taste your new and your old claret, I have been down in the cellar; there are about nine bottles old and five dozen of new. Reneaud (the housekeeper) says Dr. Digby drank nothing but Port, and his wife nothing but jelly.

Selwyn had just lent his house to the Digbys for their honeymoon. Gilly wrote again after he had sampled the Claret and highly approved of its quality.

'Your wine,' he said, 'is incomparable; Cadogan can't beat it.'

Cadogan was probably Lord Cadogan, one of Selwyn's set at White's, the great Tory club in Saint James's Street; for two years later Gilly writes from that club to Selwyn to congratulate him on landing in England and says,

When we meet, I hope you will drown all your cares in a cup of Cadogan's old claret.

From what has gone before it might seem that Selwyn's interest was Claret and good old Claret at that, but that same year we find Gilly writing again, this time about Lord Lisburne's appointment to the Admiralty.

Lord Lisburne has an excellent house in Grosvenor Square, and some of the best old claret I ever drank; but your mouth, I suppose, is altogether for Burgundy.

It seems possible that the suggestion that Selwyn's palate demands Burgundy may be connected with a curious idea expressed by Horace Walpole in a letter two years earlier that the sea

softens and makes palatable any potion as it does claret,

and one finds among the letters of the time references to what we should now regard as a superstition that the red wine of Bordeaux was improved by its journey across the Channel, so that the visitor to France would be disappointed by its aroma in its native place and was wiser to drink Burgundy. Selwyn was at the time in France.

Certainly Lord Carlisle had no confidence in Selwyn's judgment of Claret. He writes from Florence to the Wit 'in Chesterfield Street, London':

I wish your would speak to Foxcroft, in case he should have a pipe of exceeding good claret, to save it for me. I do not mean that you shall have anything to do in choosing it for me, for you can drink ink and water if you are told it is claret. Get somebody who understands it to taste it for you.

The same correspondent seems uneasy about Selwyn's taste for Burgundy, as when the latter had inflammation of the eyes, he writes,

As you have put Burgundy into your inside, I shall not be surprised to hear you have put aquafortis into your eyes.

and goes on to suggest that he will lose his sight by drinking Port and Punch with his electors at Gloucester, the seat for which he sat for many years. Later he says that if Selwyn contrives to drink Burgundy, he will be as blind as Sir J. Fielding, the blind half-brother of the author of *Tom Jones*, who succeeded him as chief magistrate in Westminster.

Undoubtedly Selwyn had a liking for red wine; for in 1771 Lord Carlisle says that he accounts for his friend's headache after dinner with Lord Clermont by supposing that he drank all the red wine within his reach, while the party was discussing horses, the Wit evidently not being interested in races. Again the Earl writes to him the following year warning him against hazard and a certain noble gambler:

Do you take care of yourself? or do you sleep between two doors? drink all the red wine you can get, and eat all the nastiness in London? Pray go home soon.

He seems to regard it as equally unwholesome to sleep in a draught, drink red wine, and eat rich food!

Another friend of Selwyn's—and they were countless—Lord March, who was to become the notorious Duke of Queensberry, seems to have had more confidence in the Wit's palate than Carlisle. He writes to Selwyn in France:

Get me the best Chambertin you can, and you may give any price for it. Chavigny I should think will be able to advise you as well as anybody.

In another letter he says:

Pray do not forget my *vin de Chambertin*; I only desire a packet of sixty bottles; send it direct to Calais.

Carlisle at any rate seems to have received his 'pipe of claret' safely, as he acknowledges the 'vin de grave.'

Another friend, Anthony Morris Storer,

a man whose singular felicity it was to excel in everything he set his heart and hand to,

86

was evidently a Claret-lover and trusted in Selwyn's judgment. We find him writing in 1774,

> If Brooks pays you for my *vin de grave* he will be more gracious than I should imagine he would be for he has not a farthing of mine in his hands; and indeed in this respect he differs very little from anybody else I know; but, as long as I am only a pauper *in meo ore*, I assure you I shall have a bottle of *vin de grave*, though it does cost four shillings a bottle. You will get by your edition of Madame de Sévigné's letters enough to pay for as much *vin de grave* as ever she drank *en Bretagne*.

Brooks, of course, is that Brooks whose name is preserved in Brooks's Club, which has never lost the glamour of Charles Fox's personality. Storer's letter provides an early reference to this former wine merchant and money-lender as club proprietor; for he had just taken over Almacks, then in Pall Mall, moving to Saint James's Street a few years later. In that age of gambling and impecunious, though potentially enormously rich, noblemen, the running of a club was a risky business, and Brooks seems to have been more guileless than his previous experience would appear to warrant; for he died in poverty in 1782, and perhaps did pay for Storer's wine, though he ran no great risk in that, since Selwyn's correspondent was the son of a West Indian magnate and when he spoke of pauperism qualified it with the Latin tag. It seems not to have been mere irony that inspired Tickell, the Wit who threw himself from a window at Hampton Court and broke his neck, to write:

> . . . liberal Brooks, whose speculative skill
> Is hasty credit and a distant bill;
> Who, nursed in clubs, disdains a vulgar trade,
> Exults to trust, and blushes to be paid.

They certainly did many things and had many ideas in the eighteenth century which seem to us very odd two hundred years later. The French Riviera would seem to me one of the last places in Europe where one would yearn for porter and strong beer, particularly if one was a Claret-lover, as we have said the Earl of Carlisle was. Yet in 1786 he writes from Nice,

We have porter and strong beer by the English ships, which are real comforts.

Charles Fox in Paris a couple of years later seems to have had no such yearnings after our insular flesh-pots, though he has more to say for the wine than the food. One is apt to forget that he was a great-great-grandson of Charles II, through his mother Lady Caroline Lennox, and it is amusing to find him claiming Charles Fitzjames, son of the Duke of Berwick, the natural son of James II by Arabella Churchill, sister of the great Duke of Marl-borough, as a cousin.

Quantities of cousins visit us; amongst the rest the Duke of Berwick. What an animal it is! I supped last night with Lauzun, Fitzjames, and some others, at what they call a *Clob à l'Anglaise*. It was in a *petite maison* of Lauzun's. There was Madame Briseau and two other women. The supper was execrably bad. However the champagne and tokay were excellent; notwith-standing which the fools made *ponche* with bad rum. This club is to meet every Saturday either here or at Versailles; I am glad to see that we cannot be foolisher in point of imitation than they are.

In the same letter Fox speaks of General Sir John Irwin as cutting the principal figure in English society in the French capital. This highly decorative and exceedingly extravagant carpet knight had been Commander-in-Chief in Ireland, and had distinguished himself by entertaining the Lord Lieutenant at a banquet in which the principal feature of the dessert was

a representation of the forces of Gibraltar invested by the Spanish forces, executed in confectionery. It exhibited a faithful view of that celebrated Rock so dear to the English nation; together with the works, batteries and artillery of the besiegers, which threw sugar plums against the walls. The expense of this osten-tatious piece of magnificence did not fall short of fifteen hundred pounds.

His place here is justified by a remark of his that illustrates the emphasis laid on quantity rather than quality by the wine-lover of the day. He was a great favourite with George III, who once remarked to him,

'They tell me, Sir John, that you love a glass of wine.'
'Those,' replied the General, 'who so informed Your Majesty, have done me great injustice: they should have said a bottle.'

The unhappy creditors of extravagant noblemen found little sympathy among their contemporaries. The Reverend Dr. Warner, one of Selwyn's closest friends and 'toadies,' tells of the seizure of the goods of Lord Foley, who, as the heirloom property could not be touched, lost little of value except two hundred dozen of choice French wine, though he and his wife had all their clothes taken.

'All this,' says Dr. Warner, 'is a monstrous good joke to the Right Honourable, who is seen laughing at it in Saint James's Street.'

He probably laughed with equal gusto at Selwyn's joke, when he fled from his creditors across the Channel;

it was a *pass-over* not much relished by the Jews.

The oddities of the time are well illustrated by the same clerical gentleman's account of a dinner he gave in 1779 to Harry Hoare, the son of the Lord Mayor, and the King's Proctor, Philip Crespigny.

The whim took them, as it sometimes will, to have a black-guard scheme of dining in my cabin, and ordering their dinner; and a very good one they had: mackarel, a delicate neck of veal, a piece of Hamborough beef, cabbage and salad, and a gooseberry tart; and when they had drank the bottle of white wine, and of port, which accompanied their dinner, and after that the only double bottle of Harry's claret that I had left, I found in an old corner (as they could not again descend to port, or, as the boys at Eton call it, black-strap) one of those two bottles of Burgundy which I took from your cellar when you gave me the key of it; and, by Jove! how they did abuse my modesty, finding it so exquisite,

89

that instead of two I did not take two dozen. But having no more, we closed the orifice of the stomach with a pint of Dantzic cherry-brandy, and have just parted in a tolerable state of insensibility to the ills of human life. Is it not good if one can forget now and then that he is a man?

There are some interesting points about this far from austere meal with its six bottles of wine and pint of liqueur between three. It is instructive to note that the boys at Eton were already familiar with Port as 'black-strap,' and a contemporary Treatise discussed at the end of this chapter throws some light on what they meant by it. Again the reference to 'the double bottle of Harry's Claret' deserves attention; for mention of Magnums is very rare in the letters of this period. We are glad to hear from a later letter of Warner's that Harry's Claret was 'very good, as he deals with Brown and Whiteford'; probably the Lord Mayor's son dealt with a City firm. It is not altogether surprising that as the reverend Doctor puts it, they succeeded in forgetting for a time that they were men, with an allowance of two bottles a man—Hock, Port, Claret, and Burgundy, plus a pint of Cherry Brandy between them. It is, however, rather a shock to learn that they drank the Hock and Port with the meal and went on to Claret and Burgundy, because 'they could not again descend to Port.'

There seems little doubt that this Port drunk with the meal was a fortified wine, and this odd idea—as it appears to us—that a wine which in our time is utterly out of place until the repast is over should be taken with food persisted well on into the next century. Captain Gronow gives an outline of what would be regarded in 1814 as a Grand Dinner in this country, and is not very kind to the 'mild but abortive attempts at Continental cooking' in which the English cooks indulged. For soup, mulligatawny and turtle were set before the guests. At one end of the table there would be a dish of salmon and at the other a turbot surrounded by smelts. The joint would be a saddle of mutton or a piece of roast beef, and there would be fowls, tongue, and ham to follow, with a few French dishes to garnish the *pièces de résistance*. The gallant Captain comments as follows on the banquet: 'the universally adored and ever-popular potato was produced at the earliest period of the dinner, and eaten with everything up to the moment when the sweets appeared. Our vegetables, the best in the world, were never honoured by an accompanying sauce and generally came to the table cold. A prime difficulty to overcome was the placing on your fork and finally in your mouth some half-dozen different eatables which occupied your plate at the same time. For example, your plate would contain, say, a slice of turkey, a piece of stuffing, a sausage, pickles, a slice of tongue, cauliflower, and potatoes. According to habit and custom, a judicious and careful selection from the little bazaar of good things was to be made with an endeavour to place a portion of each in your mouth at the same moment. In fact it appeared to me that we used to do all our compound cookery between our jaws.'

The dessert, which would come from Grange's or Owen's in Bond Street, would cost at least a pound a head, and not much wonder when Covent Garden was asking £2 12s. for a pineapple, three guineas a pound for grapes, 8s. a dozen for Nonpareil apples, and £1 10s. a dozen for Colmar pears. Out of season vegetables, too, could be very dear. The Grocers' Company had a standing order for quantities of green peas, when they did not cost more than four guineas a quart, but in 1814 they rose to six guineas, too dear even for a City Company. As for drink, 'the wines were chiefly Port, Sherry, and Hock; Claret and even Burgundy being then designated as *poor, thin, washy stuff*. A perpetual thirst seemed to come over people, both men and women, as soon as they tasted their soup; as from that moment everybody was taking wine with everybody else till the close of dinner; and such wine as produced that class of Cordiality which frequently wanders into stupefaction.'

91

The manners of the age demanded a maximum of alcohol in drink and in none of the letters of Horace Walpole or Selwyn's correspondence have I found a reference to a vintage year or a Château. They often drank Claret at the end of a meal at which they had been drinking Port and Hock and strangely enough they seemed to regard the latter as strong as the fortified wine of Portugal, but its niceties must have been entirely lost on their palates. Quantity not quality was their cry, and in August 1813 fifty-four Volunteers were sued for 126 bottles of Port, forty-eight ditto of Sherry, sixty-four half-crown bowls of punch, and twenty of negus, beside ale and porter, which they were said to have consumed one evening, and the jury found for the innkeeper, merely reducing the charge for the Port by sixpence a bottle.

Walpole tells us that the medical faculty were much impressed by the case of Charles Mildmay, Lord Fitzwalter, who was still alive in December 1755. He was past eighty-four, had been a great ladies' man, and according to Horace 'had scarce ever more sense than he has at present.' He had been living for many months on fourteen barrels of oysters, two dozen bottles of Port and seven bottles of Brandy a week.

The reader will remember the scene in Congreve's *Way of the World* in which Mirabell covenants with the adorable Millamant the conditions of their marriage. 'To the dominion of the tea-table I submit—but with proviso that you exceed not in your province . . . that on no account you encroach upon the men's prerogative, and presume to drink healths or toast fellows; for prevention of which I banish all foreign forces, all auxiliaries to the tea-table, as orange-brandy, all aniseed, cinnamon, citron, and Barbados waters, together with ratafia, and the most noble spirit of clary—but for cowslip wine, poppy water, and all dormitives, those I allow.'

It was inevitable that the cocktail should flourish when

92

the 'kick' of alcohol was the chief demand, and Mirabell avows himself its deadly foe. The *Drams* that were so popular in the first half of the eighteenth century were simply precursors of the cocktail and equally deleterious. 'Filthy strong-waters!' simpered the incomparable Mistress Bracegirdle-Millamant, but she was the perfection of fine ladies, not one of those whom the satirist tells us were always *a-tasting*. 'As soon as she rises, she must have a salutary dram, to keep her stomach from the colic; a whet before she eats, to procure appetite; after eating, a plentiful dose for correction; and to be sure a bottle of brandy under her bedside, for fear of fainting in the night.' The fashion, however, soon began to wane. In 1758, Walpole writes to his friend Sir Horace Mann asking him to send a case of liqueurs from Florence, but six weeks later countermands his request. 'If they are not bespoken, I will not trouble you for the case of Drams. Lord Hertford has given me some of his; the fashion is much on the decline, and never drinking any myself, these will last me long enough.'

Nevertheless drinks of a high alcoholic content with a *kick* continued popular both with and between meals for many years to come. In 1680, a protest had been raised against the importation of coffee on the ground that it was 'most useless, since it served neither for nourishment nor debauchery.' Something might be said for milk as a food, and a great deal for rum as an intoxicant, but what could be the good of an outlandish drink, which neither fed a man nor made him drunk. So ran the argument of the Coffee Prohibitionist, and if it failed to convince, the spirit that inspired it lasted. It predominated in aristocratic circles in Oxford, when the quiet and practical Shenstone, poet and farmer, was an undergraduate there in 1732. He tells of an evening that began with 'a sober little party,' which read Greek and drank water. Then he went to 'a very different party, a set of jolly, sprightly young fellows, most of them West country lads who drank ale, smoked tobacco, and sang bacchanalian catches.' Finally, he joined the party of 'the gentlemen commoners.' 'They treated me with Port wine and arrack punch, and now and then, when they had drunk so much as hardly to distinguish wine from water, they would conclude with a bottle or two of Claret. They kept late hours, drank their favourite toast on their knees, and in short were what were then called *bucks of the first head.*'

This tragic maltreatment of Claret, drunk when there was no possibility of appreciating its beauties, was widely spread and did not disappear with the Regency, though it seems to have escaped the notice of a Frenchman who in 1819 described with some malice the peculiarities of 'a public Tavern Dinner.' The diner's name had to be put down two days in advance and fifteen shillings paid at the door. 'A waiter brought soup and a heap of plates; he who was nearest took possession, and distributed it to those nearest him, before a second tureen was placed at the other end of the table, and that also disappeared before the arrival of a third. This soup is called mock turtle, that is pieces of Calves' head and Oxtails floating in the water in which they are dressed and has no flavour but pepper which had not been spared.' Apparently our French visitor was so shocked with the calves' head masquerading as turtle that he confounded two soups into one. In those happy days, there followed a profusion of roast and boiled meat, slightly marred by *vegetables boiled in water, the only sauce given to them in this country*. There was apparently no changing of plates; for as soon as the French guest had finished his plate of mock turtle it was loaded with a wing of boiled fowl, an enormous piece of roast beef, a slice of hot ham, a potato, two carrots, and leaves of boiled spinach. He was astonished to find that no one thought of drinking, 'for the English in general are not thirsty until no longer hungry.' Apple tarts, salad, and cheese came next and then the waiters placed before each diner a bottle of red wine (presumably Port) or Sherry as he preferred and bottles were removed to another room for consumption with oranges and nuts amid songs and toasts.

It was certainly not a connoisseur's world, but it was a world of plenty for those who could afford it and the British people were proud of it. When, in 1814, the Regent's daughter, Princess Charlotte, was married to the Prince of Coburg, pamphlets were published dwelling on the bridegroom's good luck in exchanging Continental penury for English abundance. He was depicted as stuffing himself with good food after starving on 'Sour Krout,' and in one print he is depicted with his bride with a huge piece of steaming roast beef on the table and foison of fine wines at his disposal. Burgundy and Champagne—no doubt still Champagne—had been decanted, but two Hock bottles of the traditional shape are standing in a wine cooler at the Prince's feet and two empty bottles show that he is doing himself well. It is to be observed that Port plays no part in his entertainment.

It was, of course, on the famous Methuen Treaty of 1703 that Port built up its reputation as the Englishman's wine. The early English traders in Oporto, who were there mainly to buy the produce of Brazil, were encouraged to import Portuguese rather than French wines by almost prohibitive preferential treatment, paying only £7 duty per tun as against £55 per tun on wines from France. André Simon in *Bottlescrew Days* disclosed the surprising historical fact that this sweeping privilege had no immediate effect on the trade in Port and it was not till a later date that as a table wine it for a time consigned into outer darkness Claret and Burgundy, as we have seen.

It was, I think, the ambassador responsible for this treaty, who appears as a gallant and wine-lover in a letter Horace Walpole wrote to his bosom friend Sir Horace Mann, British Minister in Florence, though not in connection with Port. One of Horry's admirers, Madame Grifoni, proposed to send him a food parcel of Italian hams and Florence wine, but he had no austerity to contend with and the present, which he would have had to acknowledge by some gifts of trinkets or the like, would have been more trouble than it was worth. He thanks his correspondent most particularly for having saved him from a plague of hams. 'Heaven!' he writes characteristically, 'how blank I should have looked at unpacking a great case of bacon and wine! My dear child, be my friend, and preserve me from heroic presents. I cannot possibly at this distance begin a new courtship of *regali* (Italian for *presents*); for I suppose that all those hams were to be converted into watches and toys. Now it would suit Sir Paul Methuen very well, who is a knight-errant of seventy-three, to carry on an amour between Mrs. Chevenix's shop (the toy and trinket shop of the day) and a noble cellar in Florence; but alas! I am neither old enough or young enough to be gallant.' Walpole as we have said was no wine-drinker and made no distinction between Port and Chianti.

He was mightily contemptuous about the unfashionable rawness of country bumpkins, who in the middle of the eighteenth century still stuck to their alcoholic drinks for morning refreshment and knew nothing of the charms of chocolate and coffee. When he was staying with George Montagu at Stowe, his superior wit as a man of fashion was tickled by the matutinal call of a young squire, Sir Harry Danvers, *booted and spurred, and buckskin-breeched.* The host inquired if the visiting baronet would drink any chocolate, and he received the reply, 'No, a little wine and water, if you please.' 'I suspected nothing,' writes Walpole, 'but that he had rode till he was dry.' Montagu called to his servant, 'Niccolo, get some wine and water.' Sir Harry desired that the water might be warm. 'I began to stare,' says Horry; 'Montagu understood the dialect, and ordered a negus. I had great difficulty to keep my countenance, and still more when I saw the baronet finish a very large jug indeed.' According to the *Concise Encyclopaedia of Gastronomy*, negus is simply mulled Port, and one feels with Walpole that it was hardly a suitable morning drink for an August day. The letter was written on August 4, 1753. It was followed by another letter, this time to George Montagu, his host on that occasion, twelve days later, and Horace showed himself decidedly unfeeling. In the interim Sir Harry had died. 'I am ashamed to tell you that I laughed half an hour yesterday at the sudden death of our new friend Sir Harry Danvers, *after a morning's airing*, the news call it; I suspect it was after a negus.' Later he apologizes for this mirth, excusing himself on the ground that the baronet's *wine and water a little warm* had left such a ridiculous effect upon him that even his death could not efface it. Sir Harry Danvers, of Culworth in Oxfordshire, died at the age of twenty-two.

Some light is thrown on the character of the Port that provided the unlucky baronet with his negus and was in the next generation to be called 'black-strap' by the Eton boys, by a pamphlet very kindly sent me by the *Instituto do Vinho do Porto*. It is a facsimile of *A Treatise on the Wines of Portugal*, by John Croft, member of the Factory at Oporto, and wine merchant of York, originally published in 1788. André Simon has dealt with the historical aspect of this pamphlet in *Bottlescrew Days*, and has shown that its author was quite wrong in jumping to the conclusion that the general use of Port wine in Great Britain dated from the Methuen Treaty of 1703, which provided that Portuguese wine should pay one-third less duty than French wine. Actually, the trade in wines between England and Portugal goes back to the fourteenth century, and it was not till a number of years after the Methuen Treaty that the consumption of Port in England increased materially.

Though Simon has summarily disposed of any pretensions John Croft might have as a serious historian, his Treatise

G

throws some amusing sidelights on the Port trade of his day, and we find him already complaining that the wines are not so rich and mellow as they used to be and do not keep as well. Port had been fully acclimatized in England. He tells us that 'Red Wines of a superior mellowness or body' had become, 'owing to the system of modern luxury, so much familiarized to us by custom in England and so much adapted to the taste and constitution of the Northern climates, as to become a staple commodity; and an Englishman of any descent, condition, or circumstances, cannot dispense with it after his good dinner, in the same manner as he uses a piece of Cheshire cheese for pretended digestion-sake.'

Before Port could become popular across the seas, it had to be fortified with brandy to check its fermentation and retain in the wine sufficient sugar, for the wine of the Douro, if it is allowed to ferment out, is horribly harsh and dry. This expedient was discovered and put into use between 1725 and 1730, but more was needed. Wine and alcohol shut up in the narrow limits of a bottle need time for amalgamation and for the throwing off of impurities, and if wine is to keep, bottles must be binned away on their sides. The early Port bottle was a picturesque, bulbous receptacle, and a good many years passed before the shape of the bottle was so modified that it would lie comfortably on its side. Evidently this difficulty had been overcome when Mr. Croft wrote, for he says that red Port, 'bottled and laid upon its side, will only bark, or tinge, and stick close to the bottle in the months of November and December.' He was in favour of bottling the wine four years after the vintage and keeping it in bottle for two years before use. Elsewhere, he complains that the Oporto factory 'were obliged to keep their wines so long on hand in their warehouses in Portugal, as they were not demanded in sale from England of so considerable a time, it having become the custom or fashion there to use none but the oldest Wines.'

None the less, wines did not keep as long as they used, partly on account of poor vintages and partly, it would seem, for another unexpected reason.

On my first glance at the Treatise, I was completely stumped as to the inward meaning of a Latin quotation on the title page: *Sensi ego, quum insidiis pallida vina bibi*— 'I marked him, when I drank the wine pale with treachery.' It comes from an elegy by Propertius telling how, after her funeral, the ghost of his mistress, Cynthia, visited him and reproached him and all his household with neglect and treachery. A servant must be tortured with red-hot irons, because he had given her the 'pale wine,' which presumably poisoned her. Why the worthy John Croft should start off an essay on Port with a reference to pale wine, defeated me, and the dictionary suggestion that the 'pallida vina' were wines that made people pale, on the analogy of pale death, did not make matters much clearer. Then, when I read the Treatise, I found that there was a sly, malicious point in the Latin reference, though the author's Port was rich red by treachery, not pale like Cynthia's wine. The treachery was, in point of fact, that ancient skeleton in the Port cupboard, the elderberry. Now elderberries have no business to find their way into wine, but I think I should prefer a stray elderberry giving colour to my Port to elder flower producing a Muscatelle flavour.

According to the worthy Croft, Port in its early days had to compete with Florence wine, a very highly coloured and inferior form of Chianti. The public taste demanded colour, and Port at that time was pale, 'because the red and white grapes were squeezed and jumbled together, as they promiscuously grew in the vineyards. . . . A liquor nearly the same as Red and White Port being mixed.' 'A Mr. Peter Bearsley, an Englishman, who resided at Viana as a factor, was the first who went to Oporto in the view, and for the purpose of speculating in the Port Wines; and on the road to the Wine country, at an Inn, he met with an Elder tree, whose juice he expressed, and mixed with the ordinary Wine, and found it had the effect of heightening and improving its colour.'

I am afraid that Mr. Croft was not so shocked by the strange meeting between Mr. Bearsley and an Elder tree as he should have been; for he writes, 'When too great a quantity of rain falls at the vintage, the red grape will be almost the colour of the white, and even requires the juice of the Elder to give it a proper red, though now all such sophistication of the Wine is not only strictly forbidden in Portugal, but attended even with capital punishment and confiscation of the Wine. . . . By the law of the General Company of the Douro, if an Elder tree is found in or about a vineyard, the penalty of forty shillings shall be incurred; and if any of the Berries, or expressed juice (which they term Baga) is found or discovered in any lodge or repository of Wine . . . the owner or proprietor is liable to be imprisoned at the mercy of the King. This I knew put into execution, and several Gentlemen of family and high rank in the Wine Country were sent to prison on suspicion only, some Elder Berries having been unluckily strewed in the pathway of their lodges, which might have been done through an evil design. The Portuguese, not being allowed to add the Elder Juice to their Wines, is the reason why the Port Wines either come over of late years so deficient in colour, or lose it so soon, that they will not keep properly in bottles above five years, without become pale and tawny. This, and the very small portion of brandy afforded to put in them, owing to the exorbitant price it is held up at by the Company, the sole vendors of it, is a very sufficient argument against the Port Wines being so long kept, as well as that the Vintages, for many years past, have not afforded so rich or mellow Wines as they formerly possessed.'

I have allowed Mr. Croft to tell his story in his own words, for the sake of reading between the lines. Black-strap he wanted, and had done a fine trade in the *baga* wines. He was no purist, and quite unable to share the gratitude of the modern wine-drinker to the Portuguese monopoly, which put an embargo on the elderberry and compelled wine-grower and wine-maker to improve their wines and vinification in order to produce such wines as the British public demanded, without fraud or adulteration.

VII

Dr. Opimian, Dr. Folliott, and the Author's Great-Grandmother

THERE has been of late a surprising revival in the popularity of Trollope's novels and, thanks partly to the wireless, Barsetshire has become almost as familiar as the Pickwick Club, after many years of oblivion. It is said that this renewal of interest may be attributed to the complete dissimilarity between the atmosphere of Trollope's world and that in which we live. If that is so, we may hope for a similar resurrection of Peacock's novels, which should be dear to the heart of every wine-lover, since their scene is set in a world of ease and plenty, troubled only by the shadows of the bad scientific age which the author saw approaching. Professor Saintsbury has been chosen as the patron saint of wine-lovers, and it would be only fair to couple with his name that of Doctor Opimian, Peacock's most famous character, of whom the author was himself the model.

'A most odd combination of sincerity, satire, cynicism, and romance,' Peacock is described in *The Concise Cambridge History of Literature*, and Dr. Opimian certainly ought to live with Meredith's Dr. Middleton, the two being tragically connected, since Peacock's daughter married the author of *The Egoist*, and their issue was *Modern*

102

Love. Dr. Opimian's love of wine is indicated by his name, and he is introduced into the novel *Gryll Grange* by two of the classical quotations that Peacock loved: first, two lines from *Alcaeus,* which he translates:

> Moisten your lungs with wine. The dog-star's sway
> Returns, and all things thirst beneath his ray;

and then a few words from *Petronius,* the Arbiter of Elegance: '*Alas! Alas! exclaimed Trimalchio. Thus wine lives longer than man! Wherefore, let us sing "Moisten your lungs. Wine is life."* '

To these quotations I will add one from Pliny concerning the year 121 B.C., in which L. Opimius was Consul. 'There was such a blaze of hot weather that in that year the grapes were literally cooked—cooking is the technical word—by the sun, and the wines made last to this day after nearly two hundred years.' Trimalchio, it will be remembered, was host at a banquet in which glass bottles labelled *Falernian Opimian* were presented.

Theophilus Opimian, a Doctor of Divinity, and the incumbent of Ashbrook-cum-Ferndale, on the outskirts of the New Forest, and therefore presumably Peacock himself, was in appearance just such a wine-loving man of letters as we would have him. Wordsworth's question, in his *Poet's Epitaph:*

> Art thou a man of purple cheer,
> A rosy man, right plump to see?

might have been answered in the affirmative by Dr. Opimian. 'His cellar was well stocked with a selection of the best vintages, under his own especial charge. . . . From the master and mistress to the cook, and from the cook to the tom cat, there was about the inhabitants of the vicarage a sleek and purring rotundity of face and figure that denoted community of feelings, habit and diet; each in its kind, of course, for the Doctor had his Port, the cook her ale, and the cat his milk, in sufficiently liberal allowance.'

From the foregoing, it might be expected that the Doctor would prove to be like Dr. Middleton essentially a Port man, but we find him at a dinner-party drinking Claret, while another of the guests was pronouncing a eulogium on the Port. Despite a taste that seems as catholic as Saintsbury's, it is Madeira that plays the greatest part in Dr. Opimian's life as we know it. In the first chapter we find him discoursing on Palestine Soup, a curiously complicated misnomer.

'We have an excellent old vegetable, the artichoke, of which we eat the head; we have another of subsequent introduction, of which we eat the root, and which we also call artichoke, because it resembles the first in flavour, though *me judice* a very inferior affair. This last is a species of the helianthus, or sunflower genus of the *Syngenesia frustranea* class of plants. It is therefore, a girasol or turn-to-the-sun. From this girasol we have made Jerusalem, and from the Jerusalem artichoke we make Palestine soup.'

It need not be said that this misnomer gives an opportunity to Peacock to express many quaint and original opinions on the misnomers of the day, and Doctor Opimian is only checked by his host's offer of 'a glass of old Madeira, which, I really believe, is what it is called.' *In vino veritas*, says the Doctor. So far as *Gryll Grange* can be said to have a hero, its *jeune premier* is Mr. Algernon Falconer, a young man who dwells in a tower, where he is waited upon by seven chaste and beautiful maidens. He seems to have no trouble with the servant problem, as these damsels had only to wait on him, pour out his wine and make music, being the regulating spirits of the household, with a staff of their own for the coarser and harder work.

Despite this charming retinue, Mr. Falconer falls in love with the lady of Gryll Grange and begins drinking Madeira like anything to keep up his spirits. Dining alone, he drank a bottle of Madeira as if it had been so much water. For some days Madeira was to him 'like ale to the Captain and his friends in Beaumont and Fletcher (*The Scornful Lady*), almost his eating and his drinking solely.' He drinks the same wine all through dinner when the Doctor is dining with him, and after dinner calls for another bottle, while his guest is content with a bottle of Claret. 'The more his mind was troubled, the more Madeira he could drink without disordering his head.' Madeira, poured by two of his lovely Hebes, served as an approximation to Helen's Nepenthe, an antidote to intense vexation of spirit, and Peacock transfers to this wine an Italian song written in honour of a Tuscan wine.

'It is the true potable gold, which straightway banishes every ill without remedy. It is Helen's Nepenthe which makes the world joyful, for ever free and immune from dark and gloomy thoughts.'

Peacock is singularly chary about giving particulars of the wines mentioned copiously in his pages, and Madeira is just Madeira, so that we cannot tell whether he was thinking of Malmsey, Sercial or Boal. It had been the great age of Madeira—a fashion started, André Simon tells us, by the First Gentleman in Europe, afterwards known as George IV—but the end had come.

Gryll Grange was published in 1861 and it is rather surprising to find in it no reference to the disaster that had just befallen this glorious wine. In August 1860 a firm of shippers issued a circular announcing that the island of Madeira could no longer be numbered among wine-growing countries. Nine-tenths of the vines had been destroyed by oidium or rooted up and the remainder were very sickly. In 1851, 30,000 pipes, each of ninety-two gallons, had been produced, and for the next ten years no wine was made. One can only suppose that the author, Doctor Opimian and all his friends had been fortunate enough to lay down sufficient stocks of Madeira to be able to depend on their cellars for the rest of their lives. At least they were born too early to see phylloxera descend on the vineyards as soon as they were partially restored from oidium.

I am glad to say that Dr. Opimian was exceedingly partial to Claret and it is aggravating on his part to keep to himself the names and vintages of the wines which gave him such satisfaction. On one occasion, grievously discomposed by a carriage accident in a thunderstorm, he indulged in a declamation against the electric telegraph, which he accused of increasing human misery, and having in this way somewhat soothed his troubled spirit, 'he propitiated his Genius by copious libations of Claret, pronouncing high panegyrics on the specimen before him, and interspersing quotations in praise of wine as the one great panacea for the cares of the world.'

The full discussion of an interesting topic after dinner we are told might well exhaust a good bin of Claret. Such discussions must not interfere with, but promote, the circulation of the bottle. Each speaker must push on the bottle with as much energy as he spoke with, and it seems that those who were silent 'swallowed the wine and the opinion together, as if they relished them both.' Professor Saintsbury was always in favour of enjoying Claret in the fashion of our ancestors, when the meal was over, and Doctor Opimian insists that he has always found discussion very absorbent of Claret.

At this point a confession is forced upon the *laudator temporis acti*; it seems certain that Doctor Opimian's appreciation of Claret differed widely from our own and that may be the reason why he has nothing to say about Châteaux and vintages. Professor Saintsbury tells us that he had lived through two or three different phases of attitude to the temperature at which Claret should be drunk. 'There was the Ice Age—certainly a barbarous time.' Readers of Browning will remember how, in *Bishop Blougram's Apology*, the Bishop begins with a kind of coo of satisfaction over his Claret, 'cool i'faith!' and later tells Mr. Gigadibs,

Try the cooler jug,
Put back the other, but don't jog the ice.

'Very harrowing!' says the Professor, 'icing good Claret at all is barbarous; but the idea of subjecting it to processes of alternate freezing, thawing and freezing again is simply Bolshevist.' Every modern connoisseur would, I think, agree that all the finer points and subtler delicacies of the bouquet and aroma of a good Claret are imperceptible if the wine is drunk very cold. It becomes just a beverage *pour la soif*, and I am afraid that Dr. Opimian's attitude to Claret for all his eulogies of its excellence lacked that discrimination which is only possible when the wine is at its optimum temperature. For when he lunched for the first time with Mr. Falconer, Madeira and Sherry were on the table (this is the only reference to Sherry in *Gryll Grange*; it was long before light, dry Sherries were thought of) and the attendant Hebes offered him Hock and Claret.

'The Doctor took a capacious glass from each of the fair cup-bearers, and pronounced both wines excellent and deliciously cool. He declined more . . . not to infringe his anticipations of dinner.' Again, when he is dining with his friends at Gryll Grange, the chapter is headed by some Greek verses bidding Doris cool the wine, and we are told that they dined well as usual, and drank their wine cool.

Punch played an important part in the festivities of that generation, and Dr. Opimian counts the inexhaustible bowl of punch among the delights of Christmas, which also includes the gigantic sausage, the baron of beef, the vast globe of plum-pudding and the tapping of the old October. At a Twelfth-Night celebration, the gentlemen, who had not had their usual allowance of wine after an early dinner, remained at the supper table over a bowl of punch which had been provided in ample quantity, and, in the intervals of dancing, was not absolutely disregarded even by the young ladies. In this connection, Peacock quotes a Goldoni comedy in which a gentleman with the attractive name of

107

Lord Runebif meets a masked lady on the terrace of a Venetian café. He offers her coffee or chocolate, but she refuses him, only allowing herself to be tempted when he suggests punch. When she accepts, he remarks, 'Then she is English.' Peacock observes that he does not offer her tea, which, as a more English drink, might have entered into rivalry with punch, especially if it is drunk with arrack, as it is in another comedy of Goldoni's.

It may be imagined that Peacock did not love the totallers, and he devotes a page to their scarification. 'A teetotaller! Well! He is the true Heautontimorumenos, the self-punisher, with a jug of toast-and-water for his Christmas wassail. So far his folly is merely pitiable, but his intolerance makes it offensive. He cannot enjoy his own tipple unless he can deprive me of mine. . . . He is like Bababec's *faquir*, who sat in a chair full of nails *pour avoir de la considération*. But the *faquir* did not want˙ others to do the same. He wanted all the consideration for himself, and kept all the nails for himself. If these meddlers would do the like by their toast-and-water, nobody would begrudge it them.'

Repasts called Siberian dinners, 'where you just look on fiddle-faddles, while your dinner is behind a screen, and you are served with rations like a pauper,' seem to have been the fashion, and Dr. Opimian is very definite that a sirloin of beef is in its proper place, not on a side-table, but in front of the host, quoting Addison in the *Tatler*.

'Upon turning my head I saw a noble sirloin on the side-table, smoking in the most delicious manner. I had recourse to it more than once, and could not see without some indignation that substantial English dish banished in so ignominious a manner to make way for French kickshaws.'

Gryll Grange concludes with Dr. Opimian celebrating nine marriages, the heroes and the heroines and all the Hebes being satisfactorily paired off, and presiding over a terrific wedding breakfast. Here we have the only mention of Champagne, and its appearance is noteworthy, since the popping of the corks seems to have been at least as important as the contents of the bottles. Dr. Opimian's speech wound up with the following peroration: 'And now, to the health of the brides and bridegrooms in bumpers of Champagne. Let all the attendants stand by, each with a fresh bottle, with only one uncut string. Let all the corks, when I give the signal, be discharged simultaneously; and we will receive it as a peal of Bacchic ordnance, in honour of the Power of Joyful Event, a Roman deity, *invocato hilaro atque prospero Eventu*, whom we may assume to be presiding on this auspicious occasion.'

Dr. Opimian is certainly the most famous of Peacock's characters. Does not Professor Saintsbury mention him in the same breath as Mr. Pickwick among the great men of fiction? The Doctor had an amiable weakness of taking his brandy at night with hot water in winter and soda-water in summer, and the Professor expresses the hope that he made a point of keeping the brown brandy for the purpose rather than pale, as the author of *Notes on a Cellar-Book* holds it better as a liqueur and very much better for 'the composition of that grand old stuff,' hot brandy and water. *De coloribus non est disputandum*, especially when they are dependent on caramel. In *Crotchet Castle*, an earlier novel than *Gryll Grange*, we find another clerical Deipnosophist, the Reverend Doctor Folliott, 'a gentleman,' we are told, 'endowed with a tolerable stock of learning, an interminable swallow, and an indefatigable pair of lungs.'

In these days of austerity, some may find a nostalgic pleasure in looking at Dr. Folliott breakfasting at Crotchet Castle—the book was published in 1831—and beginning to 'compose his spirits by the gentle sedative of a large cup of tea, the demulcent of a well-buttered muffin and the tonic of a small lobster.' 'A man of taste,' he soliloquized, 'is seen at once in the array of his breakfast-table. . . . Chocolate, coffee, tea, cream, eggs, ham, tongue, cold fowl, all these are good, and bespeak good knowledge in him who sets them forth: but the touchstone is fish; anchovy is the first step, prawns and shrimps the second; and I laud him who reaches even to these; potted char and lampreys are the third, and a fine stretch of progression; but lobster is, indeed, matter for a May morning, and demands a rare combination of knowledge and virtue in him who sets it forth.' A Scottish guest breaks in with a claim for a fine fresh trout, hot and dry, in a napkin, or a herring out of the water into the frying-pan on the shore of Loch Fyne.

The Amphitryon of the breakfast, Mr. Crotchet was a financier of Hebrew and Caledonian origin, who possessed an inborn love of disputation and entertained largely for the pleasure of hearing people argue and arguing himself. He is recommended to us by Dr. Folliott for his cellar; for we learn from him that in that temple of Bacchus lay a thousand dozen of old wine, 'a beautiful spectacle, I assure you, and a model of arrangement.' One of Mr. Crotchet's guests was obsessed by a phobia of water, which he believed to cause not only malaria but also every disease under the sun, and the divine insisted that the propinquity of wine is a matter of much more importance than the longinquity of water against which it was a talismanic antidote.

From our point of view, the chief interest of *Crotchet Castle* lies in the account of a great dinner party with a remarkable assortment of wine given to eighteen people, if I have counted correctly. So far as I can judge, the wines were served with almost barbaric variety, and in a haphazard array that would dismay the heart of the modern connoisseur. I spoke of the prominent part played by Madeira in the annals of Gryll Grange, though oidium had already ravaged the vineyards and made further supplies more than problematic. Mr. Crotchet was providing his guests with the finest Madeira at a time when those island wines were at the topmost peak of their glory, never again to be equalled, and we find at the dinner party Dr. Folliott starting with Madeira. In those hard-drinking days, the *apéritif* and deleterious cocktail were still unthought of, and perhaps our author gives us a hint as to their origin in his description of the party in the drawing-room, 'during the miserable half-hour before dinner, when dullness reigns predominent over the expectant company, especially when they are waiting for some one last comer, whom they all heartily curse in their hearts, and whom, nevertheless, or indeed therefore-the-more, they welcome as a sinner, more heartily than all the just persons who had been punctual to their engagement.'

After smacking his lips over the fine music of the clinking of plates, the refreshing shade of the dining-room and the elegant fragrance of the roast, Dr. Folliott lays down the law: 'A glass of wine after soup is, as the French say, the *verre de santé*. The current of opinion sets in favour of Hock: but I am for Madeira; I do not fancy Hock till I have laid a substratum of Madeira.' As was clear in *Gryll Grange*, Madeira, which owes its existence to the enterprise of an Englishman who started the wine industry there in 1745, had become the wine of all work like Sherry has been in our time, to be drunk at any time of the day and with any part of the meal. In our view, the choice between a glass of Madeira and a glass of Hock, as though one could stand a substitute for the other, sounds more than curious. Madeira should certainly have provided a solid, not to say heavy and dangerous, foundation for the long lists of wines to follow.

After his Madeira, Dr. Folliott played with some salmon, a salmon caught in the Thames that very May morning, in preference to a turbot that flanked it. Then he proceeded to his glass of Hock, but, alas! not a word is said as to its vineyard and provenance. Apparently he was still playing with his salmon when the son of the house offered Champagne. At least he had just terrified his neighbour, the love-sick and far from intellectual Captain Fitzchrome, by suggesting that he remembered a passage in *Athenaeus*, where he cites Menander on the subject of fish-sauce. 'The science of fish-

111

sauce,' the Doctor declared, 'is by no means brought to perfection; a fine field of discovery still lies open in that line.' Oyster and lobster sauce were the pillars of Hercules, but he craved for cruet sauces, 'where the quintessence of the sapid is condensed in a phial.' ·

The worthy Doctor did not refuse Champagne; indeed there is no trace of his 'interminable swallow' refusing anything good to drink, but he puts a curious condition to his acceptance. 'You will permit my drinking it when it sparkles. I hold it a heresy to let it deaden in my hand, while the glass of my *compotator* is being filled on the opposite side of the table.' I mentioned this passage to André Simon and he approved Dr. Folliott's appreciation of the sparkle, remarking that the Champagne firms had to take endless pains to put it in the wine and it would be absurd to waste it. I reminded him of days not so long ago, when in many Paris restaurants the client was provided with a wooden instrument, first cousin I think to the American swizzle stick employed for the mixing of cocktails, in order that he might revolve it in his glass and swish all the sparkle out of the wine. The makers of useless and expensive gadgets for the viciously extravagant produced gold jewelled tools for the same purpose. It does seem ridiculous to suppress the special characteristic of a wine, which demands so much trouble and expense for its making, but I have heard many ladies complain that the sparkle gave them hiccoughs, and for myself I do like my Champagne to be so old that the rather embarrassing vigour of youth has worn itself off. No doubt the sparkle and the pop of corks does make for gaiety, but I should personally deprecate the firing of a salute with Champagne bottles such as that described in *Gryll Grange*. Those who set special store on Champagne being 'up' are wont to sing the praises of Dom Perignon as the inventor of sparkling wine through the reintroduction of the cork, as though it was a startling innovation in the history of wine-making. In point

112

of fact, wine-growers must have been familiar with wine that sparkled from the days of Noah; for all enclosed wine becomes effervescent with carbonic acid gas, if its fermentation has not been complete. Varro says that a cellar should have a floor sloping down to a tank, which collects the wine that may excape from the *dolia* burst by secondary fermentation, and I remember a cellar at Frascati where wine bottled too early had blown out half the bottle-corks and was as fizzy as ginger-beer.

It appears that Champagne as a sparkling wine had to be poured by a servant. The hero of *Gryll Grange* had all his wines poured by his virtuous and beautiful Hebes. At Crotchet Castle, however, there must have been an array of decanters on the table perpetually circulating in no particular order. Peacock uses a verb that I often heard in my youth, and it is still current in Oxford Colleges, to 'buz' the bottle as an instruction to empty the decanter.

We next find Dr. Folliott with Vin de Grave which was presumably white, as it was immediately followed by a glass of Sauternes. Then comes Hermitage: 'Nothing better,' says the Doctor. 'The father who first chose the solitude of that vineyard, knew well how to cultivate his spirit in retirement.' It is rather surprising that Peacock with his wealth of learning on the most out-of-the-way subjects did not know that the legendary Hermit of Hermitage was not a Father but a Crusader.

After the Hermitage Dr. Folliott has a glass of wine—its origin unspecified—with each of the young ladies: and it is when the last course and the dessert have been taken away that he reaches the crown of the feast with a wine that calls from him the exclamation, 'Matchless Claret, Mr. Crochet!' 'Vintage of fifteen' is the reply. I have no records of Claret that go back to 1815, but we have all heard of Waterloo Port, and it seems clear that Waterloo Claret must have been equally remarkable. It cannot have been more than fifteen years old when the Doctor was drinking it and

113   H

one may assume that it was of a rich dark colour, since he expressed himself in favour of seeing the world through his wineglass, full of Claret. 'Then you see both darkly and brightly.'

The dinner ended with a musician guest leading a chorus:

> We'll dine and drink, and say if we think
> That any thing better can be,
> And when we have dined, wish all mankind
> May dine as well as we. . . .
> On the brilliant dreams of our hopeful schemes
> The light of the flask shall shine;
> And we'll sit 'till day, but we'll find the way
> To drench the world with wine.

If tradition speak true my great-grandfather, Dr. George Augustus Lamb, D.D., Rector of Iden near Rye, might have sat as a model for Dr. Opimian. He was one of that family of Lambs who were regularly Mayors of Rye in the eighteenth and early nineteenth centuries, and in virtue of this office Barons of the Cinque Ports, with the privilege of holding a canopy over the Sovereign's head in the Coronation Procession. Their house, a show place of the little town, its beautiful garden house wrecked by enemy action, was once the home of Henry James and later that of E. F. Benson. My great-grandmother, Julia Louisa Lamb, may count as a contemporary of Peacock, since she started her big Recipe Book in 1827, and some of her recipes may serve as illustrations of the life and manners so graphically described in Peacock's novels. She was the daughter of Dr. Edward Bancroft, an American who seems to have had some difficulty in making up his mind on which side to fight in the War of Independence, as he was accused of being a spy in the pay of both parties. A Fellow of the Royal Society, he invented an aniline dye which brought him wealth, and was a friend of Paul Jones and Benjamin Franklin, with whose mission he went to Paris in the days of the Revolution. He bought a French privateer to prey on British merchantmen under the American flag, but she was captured by a British frigate as soon as she put her nose outside Cherbourg, and the American Government steadfastly refused to pay for her. Tradition says that he attended Louis XVI to the scaffold, and he was certainly on good enough terms with the Royal Family to leave his descendants intimate relics of the tragedy.

His daughter's recipes show that she was a good linguist, for a number of them are in French or German, and some seem to mark the engagement of foreign governesses, notably a Belgian from Liége and a German from the Rheingau. One notices that in those happy days French brandy was an ever-present stand-by for the cook, and the generosity with which it is prescribed must not blind us to the fact that it represents far more than the same quantity today at thirty under proof. The smugglers no doubt brought it over with very high alcoholic strength to save bulk, and I am afraid that the popularity of French brandy at Iden parsonage was not unconnected with the smuggling trade; for there are several family legends concerning the running of contrabrand cargoes near Rye.

Brandy was the essential ground of that popular cordial, Shrub, which Mrs. Lamb made in the following way:

'To nine quarts of brandy put two quarts of lemon juice and four pounds of loaf sugar, infuse half the lemon peals in the brandy twenty-four hours, then put it into a cask that holds nearly or exactly the quantity, let it be well rolled and jumbled about, once a day, for four or five days. Then let it stand till it be fine, and then bottle it off. . . . A few oranges will do well among the lemons. . . . N.B.— The above receipt is right, if you would make it rich and good; if you would make it poorer, then you must put in more brandy. It generally fines in ten or twelve days, but it should not be bottled till it be perfectly fine.'

Great-grandmama's observation: 'Shrub is much better made half of brandy and half of rum.'

I do not know who my great-grandmother's great-grandmother may have been—she must have been born in the century in which Shakespeare died—with her connoisseurship of Shrub, but I suspect she must have been on the Lamb side of her family, as they were noted for their love of good living.

Next to Shrub, we have Milk Punch, which was made in even larger quantities:

'Twenty quarts of brandy put into the peal of twenty-four Seville oranges and twenty-four lemons pared very thin, let them infuse twelve hours, then have ready thirty quarts of water boiled and cooled, with fifteen pounds of treble refined sugar, mix the water and brandy together adding the juice of thirty Seville oranges and of twenty-four lemons, strain it off from the peal, add to it a quart of new milk and barrel it, bring it down close and let it stand for a month or six weeks, then bottle it, and it will keep many years, the older the better.'

'A Recipe to make Cardinal,' which I attribute to the German governess, raises a problem. Cardinal does not appear in the *Concise Encyclopaedia of Gastronomy*, but Professor Saintsbury says it is 'only a rather silly name for mulled claret.' To my great-grandmother, it seems to have meant something quite different, to judge from the recipe:

'Four bottles of light Rhine wine. One bottle of strong white wine and one bottle of strong red wine: sugar to the taste, but half a pound, the very outside to the above quantity of wine. Two pomeranzins about the size of a pigeon's egg to be peeled very thin, and put together into a glass of water or light wine for four hours before the Cardinal is wanted, the thin part only to be put into it.

N.B.—The pomeranzins must be taken out after they have infused four hours—and if peeled *thick*, give *headache*.'

Nothing is said about the mulling of this liquid. As for the pomeranzins, pomeranze appears to be German for an orange, and I suppose the pomeranzin of the size of a pigeon's egg must be a mandarin orange, though why it should give anyone a headache I cannot imagine.

Cool Tankard, a very mixed liquor, also lacks the appeal necessary for inclusion in the Wine and Food Society's publication, and I cannot say I am surprised, as appreciation of beer and wine combined nowadays demands an exceptional palate.

'Strew sugar and grated nutmeg over a toast, and soak in the juice of two lemons, having first rubbed some lumps over the rinds to take off the essence of the peels; then add to these a little borage, a handful of balm, a few juniper berries and a sprig or two of young lavender tops. Three pints of good table beer and the same quantity of any sort of white wine. A glass of brandy and a glass of Capillaire will improve it.'

As a home-made liqueur, we have a recipe for Crême de Noyau, which may have tasted nicer than it sounds:

'Make a syrup with two wine quarts of spring water and two pounds of loaf sugar, pour it into a gallon of brandy. Add three pints of milk boiled—the rinds of five lemons, half a pound of bitter almonds, blanched and bruised—put it all into a large stone jar—let it stand four or five days. Shake the jar for some time every day—then filter through blotting paper and bottle for use. It may be drank [sic] in a month, but it greatly improves by keeping.'

'Dr. Meade's Syllabub' is something far more elaborate than the Syllabub of the Wine and Food Society's *Encyclopaedia*:

'Supposing the bowl to hold three quarts (presumably of fresh rich milk), mix a pint and a quarter of Port wine, half a pint of Hock, and half a pint of Mountain, with thirteen ounces of loaf sugar, half a large lemon—two small spoonsfull of vinegar and nutmeg to your taste—and three large spoonsfull of brandy.'

There was little danger of my great-grandfather allowing

117

his best Port to be diverted to the composition of Syllabub; for it is told of him that he went down to his cellar every day of his life and with his own hands brought up a Magnum of Port, carrying it with infinitely greater care than he would have bestowed on any of his babies. This Magnum he would share with any visitor, or drink himself, if fate compelled.

In those happy days brandy could be spared for the making of ginger wine and even 'For washing silks, sattins, ribbons, blondes, etc., of every description and colour,' a pint of it mixed with six ounces of honey and two ounces of soft soap. It played no part, however, in 'Prince Esterhazy's Ambrosia for the Breath,' which consists of a mixture of terra japonica, sugar-candy, ambergris, musk, gum tragacanth and orange flower water. Though they were prodigal with some commodities that are rarities with us, thrift was still held in high esteem, and they agreed with the French that there were no such things as small economies. The good housewife did not forget 'a secret in buying.' 'Buy in winter, and sell in summer liquids that are sold by measure. Thirty-two gallons bought in winter will make thirty-three in summer, as all fluid bodies contract with cold and expand with heat.'

There are specifics for all kinds of ailments and accidents, and toothache cures abound, with chilblains a good second. For a bruise on the eye, the application of conserve of red roses or the pulp of a rotten apple in a fold of old cambric is recommended. For styptics to check bleeding, you can take your choice between the outside woof of silk-worms and bruised nettle-leaves. A fearsome potion for rheumatism composed of turpentine, aloes and sal volatile, has, we are assured, cured many very bad cases.

I have passed over many cooking recipes which would be very attractive, if this England of ours was still abundantly provided with eggs, poultry and cream, but in present circumstances they would be tantalizing rather than amusing. I wind up with a puzzle with which quite unfairly I stumped André Simon the other day. What is bandoline? My great-grandmother says it is made by soaking the crushed pips of a ripe quince for twenty-four hours in water and adding a little rum and perfume. Simon naturally thought it was something to drink, as I did, until I found in Larousse that it was nothing of the kind, but just a gummy kind of hairwash to keep the parting in place.

VIII

Headaches, Soda-Water, and a Lever Banquet

*D*ON *JUAN* and *Vanity Fair* provide abundant information as to the morning after, another name for excess and its consequences, expressed in terms of soda-water and the Latin word *crapula*, which is particularly repulsive to the wine-lover whose creed is golden moderation.

> The drunkard now supinely snores,
> His load of ale sweats through his pores;
> Yet when he wakes, the swine shall find
> A crapula remains behind.

Mr. Aldous Huxley in *Texts and Pretexts* quotes this quatrain from Charles Cotton—Lamb's *hearty*, *cheerful Mr. Cotton*—with fiendish glee, expatiating on the magic effect of the word *crapula*. It certainly does seem to provide an apt description of Jos. Sedley's condition the morning after that excursion to Vauxhall Gardens, when he called Becky Sharp 'his soul's darling' four times and consumed a quart of rack punch.

'What is the rack in the punch at night,' asks Thackeray, borrowing a pun from Byron, 'to the rack in the head of a morning? To this truth I can vouch as a man; there is no headache in the world like that caused by Vauxhall punch.

Through the lapse of twenty years, I can remember the consequence of two glasses!—two wine glasses, but two, upon the honour of a gentleman; and Joseph Sedley, who had a liver complaint, had swallowed at least a quart of the abominable mixture.'

Rack one may reasonably take as a synonym of Arrack. Turning to the *Concise Encyclopaedia of Gastronomy*, Section VIII, Wine, we find it defined as 'a fiery spirit distilled chiefly in the Dutch Indies and British India, from rice. . . . Although some Arrack is much worse than others there is no Arrack pleasing to a cultivated palate.' Messrs. Berry Bros and Rudd, I believe, still possess one or two bottles of the Arrack brought back by Clive from India in the latter years of the eighteenth century. Professor Saintsbury says that Arrack was once as common in English cellars as brandy or rum and much commoner than whisky. With his catholic taste he finds a place for it in his own. 'A not disagreeable cross between rum and Irish whiskey—good enough neat, but better in the rack punch, for which it used to be chiefly employed.' No doubt he was spared acquaintance with the *Encyclopaedia's* 'worst Arrack of all,' distilled by the Tartars of Tungusia from fermented sour mare's milk.

The wireless version of *Vanity Fair* left out the most interesting point in Thackeray's picture of Sedley groaning in agonies on the sofa in his lodgings.

'Soda-water was not invented yet. Small beer—will it be believed?—was the only drink with which unhappy gentlemen soothed the fever of their previous night's potation.'

The collocation of small beer and breakfast always calls up for me a vision of Queen Elizabeth, though no doubt the beer she drank of a morning was stingo in comparison with our government-controlled swipes. When I was at Oxford, beer provided a ceremonial conclusion to those breakfasts of which I see Mr. Stephen Gwynn has been speaking in *Memories of Enjoyment*, whether they were the prescribed training breakfasts or meals of entertainment. Invitations to breakfast seem to be a rarity nowadays, though they were favoured by Lloyd George in his time, and I must admit that they scarcely provide the most suitable occasions for scintillating conversation.

Undoubtedly the aspect of breakfast must have been mightily changed by the introduction of tea and coffee, and it would now seem that the invention of soda-water had also a profound influence on our manners. Coffee appears to have attained a wider popularity than tea owing to the Coffee Houses—for tea was still considered essentially a lady's drink until the end of the nineteenth century. When I was a child, it never occurred to anyone to invite a man to a tea party, indeed my father would have regarded such an invitation as an insult. Tea was a drink he never touched, though he was a connoisseur of coffee. Soda-water was no doubt a minor novelty, but it evidently impressed Thackeray and Thackeray was a real wine-lover. Even if a lack of definition in his eulogies of Château Larose left a permanent confusion in the minds of his wine-drinking readers, he knew good wine when it came his way, and it was cruel of death in 1863 to deprive him of drinking the great 1858 Clarets.

The scene of the first chapters in *Vanity Fair* is laid between 1800 and the battle of Waterloo and not many years can have passed between Jos. Sedley's misadventure with the rack punch and the introduction of soda-water. For we find it mentioned as a common-place in the Second Canto of *Don Juan*, published in 1819.

> Let us have wine and women, mirth and laughter,
> Sermons and soda-water, the day after.

Byron made a great show of being a wine-lover, but in point of fact his tastes lay in another direction. He could write a drinking song, 'Fill the Goblet again,' but the praise of good liquor does not ring quite true, and bacchanalian merriment is a pose that does not sit well on the founder of the Byronic legend. He gives this insincerity away in his diary when he writes, 'The effect of all wines and spirits upon me is strange. It *settles*, but it makes me gloomy— gloomy at the very moment of their effect, and not gay hardly ever. But it composes for a time, though sullenly,' So his enthusiasm about

> . . . Champagne with foaming whirls,
> As white as Cleopatra's melted pearls . . .

must be taken with a grain of salt and considered rather as interesting evidence that, even in those early days of the nineteenth century, emphasis was laid upon the paleness of its colour than as a proof that Byron could be cheerful in his cups. He had, as the French say, 'the wine sad.' It is, however, instructive to note that the modern craze for very pale Champagne had its precedent.

In the circumstances, it is not surprising that Byron's most ecstatic rapture is reserved for a pick-me-up on the morning after, at the hour of sermons and soda-water. His advice is, first, 'get very drunk, and when you wake with headache, then ring for your valet—bid him quickly bring some Hock and soda-water.'

> Nor Burgundy in all its sunset glow,
> After long travel, ennui, love or slaughter,
> Vie with that draught of Hock and soda-water.

This blasphemous preference for Hock and soda on a crapulous morning over Burgundy calls for the gravest reprobation, but to pay the devil his due, the author of *Childe Harold* sometimes shows signs of grace in vinous doctrines. For in the passage we have just quoted he does say, 'Few things surpass old wine,' and that in reference to Champagne. The taste for old Champagne counts among the most refined pleasures of the connoisseur and Byron was evidently thinking of wine so old that it was more aptly described as creaming than sparkling, as the following simile demonstrates:

123

> And the small ripple spilt upon the beach
>   Scarcely o'erpass'd the cream of your Champagne,
> When o'er the brim the sparkling bumpers reach,
>   That spring-dew of the spirit! the heart's rain!

It was a time when Champagne and Hock counted among the most fashionable wines. In one of Byron's skits, Lady Bluemount starts her luncheon with a glass of Madeira, but the real attraction of the literary society to which she belongs is 'the sciences, sandwiches, Hock and Champagne' and sweet lobster salad at two hours past midnight—Hock, we may be sure undefiled with soda. Again we find Hock cheek by jowl with 'Imperial waltz! imported from the Rhine, Famed for the growth of pedigrees and wine,' the dance that was shocking everyone by the liberties it permitted.

Cognac as a *chasse-café* we all know, but as a concomitant of tea it is unknown to me, though tea with a dash of whisky in it was a short-lived craze in my undergraduate days. Byron, however, regards brandy as a useful corrective to the maudlin properties of green tea and black Bohea.

> 'Tis pity wine should be so deleterious,
> For tea and coffee leave us much more serious.
>   Unless when qualified with thee, Cogniac!
>   Sweet Naiad of the Phlegethontic rill!
> Ah! why the liver wilt thou thus attack,
>   And make, like other nymphs, thy lovers ill?

It may be well to remind the reader that Phlegethon is a river of Hell. Elsewhere, in *The Island*, Byron suggests that Brandy was 'a liquid path to epic fame,' and oddly enough attributes the slogan of 'Brandy for heroes' to Burke. Of course Dr. Johnson was responsible for this exaltation of wine-spirit. 'He was persuaded,' says Boswell, 'to take one glass of claret. He shook his head and said, "Poor stuff! No, Sir, claret is the liquor for boys; port for men; but he who aspires to be a hero" (smiling) "must drink brandy".'

An unkind commentator attaches to the poet's reflections on brandy and the liver the following quotations from his diary:

I have been considering what can be the reason why I always wake at a certain hour of the morning and always in very bad spirits—I may say in actual despair and despondency, in all respects, even of that which pleased me over night. In about an hour or two this goes off, and I compose either to sleep again, or at least to quiet. In England, five years ago, I had the same kind of hypochondria, but accompanied with so violent a thirst, that I have drunk as many as thirteen bottles of soda-water in one night, after going to bed, and been still thirsty. At present I have not the thirst, but the depression of spirits is no less violent. What is it?—*liver*? I suppose that it is all hypochondria.

Soda-water is not recorded as playing any part in the life of Byron's contemporary, John Mytton, whose biography by Nimrod ranks as one of the classics of Sport, and the Cambridge historian of English Literature calls Mytton one of the most heroic sportsmen who ever lived. I must admit that my interest in the exploits of one whom it was kind to describe as half-mad when he was sober and quite mad when he was drunk lacks enthusiasm; especially since one of his oldest friends made an affidavit that he had been continually drunk for twelve successive years, thus beating the five years' record of the then Earl of Rochester. His excesses, however, do throw light on the ways and manners of a period now nearly forgotten, and the student of wine may find matter for thought in the record of this Port-drinking. For Port was his wine from his earliest youth. He was expelled from Westminster (where he spent £800 a year or double his allowance as a ward in Chancery) and Harrow, knocked down his private tutor, and was entered on the books of both universities, but matriculated at neither and 'the only visible and outward sign of his ever intending to do so, was his ordering of three pipes of Port wine to be sent addressed to him at Cambridge.'

Port was not his only wine. We have a description of his cellar with 'hogsheads of ale, standing like soldiers in close column, and wine enough in wood and bottle for a Roman Emperor.' He made his own malt, and *John Mytton*,

Licensed Maltster, was painted over the malt-house door. His between-meals allowance of Port was from four to six bottles a day. He shaved with a bottle of Port on his table, worked steadily at it throughout the day, a glass or two at a time, probably had a bottle after lunch and drank the rest after dinner and supper. 'He is,' says Nimrod, 'a memorable example of the comparatively harmless effects of *very good wine*, which he always had, and just of a proper age—about eight years old—for assisted by exercise, such as he took, it was many years before it injured him.' Actually by some miracle he attained his thirty-eighth year and then it was brandy that ruined his constitution. Mytton died in 1834, and the story told by his biographer takes no account of vintage Port, so that he must have been drinking Port from the wood. It was said that one of his horses called Sportsman dropped down dead in his gig in consequence of his owner having given him a bottle of mulled Port at Wrexham, but Nimrod who knew the horse well does not vouch for the cause of the death. He certainly started a fashion of treating his hunters to a quart or two of warm beer.

They had queer ideas on dietetics in those days. Nimrod is really more horrified at Mytton's Gargantuan appetite for filbert nuts than for the insatiability of his thirst, and regards the combination of nuts and wine as almost worse than the drinking of eau de cologne and lavender water in which the subject of his biography sometimes indulged. Since the days of Athens nuts and wine have been associated, and the Greeks recognized the kinship between the walnut and noble dessert wine by calling it the *Karyon Basilikon*, the Royal Nut. Nimrod, however, was convinced that nuts and wine were a deadly mixture. 'It was often alarming,' he writes, 'to witness the quantity of dry nuts Mytton would eat, with the quantity of port wine which he would drink; and on my once telling him at his own table that the ill-assorted mixture caused the death of a school-fellow of mine, he carried a dish of filberts into the drawing-room

with him for the purpose of *clearing decks,* as he said.'
Though the brother of the victim of nuts and Port was
present and confirmed the story, Mytton for all his madness
was more in line with modern medical science than his well-
wishers, and continued to eat nuts with undiminished gusto.
He and a friend left London with eighteen pounds of filberts
in the carriage and devoured them all before they arrived at
his home at Halston. As he said, they sat up to their knees in
nut-shells. His chief purveyor of filberts had an unlimited
order for the purchase of them, all over the country, and
would send to Halston a couple of cart-loads in the season.

Chance willed it that I should pass from the perusal of
the barbarous and rather revolting extravagances of Mytton
to the more civilized pages of *Arthur O'Leary,* one of those
high-spirited Irish novels in which Charles Lever wrote of
the years following Mytton's death. The scene is laid in
1856. In the fifth chapter we are taken to Belgium and the
description of a *most appetizing supper* offered by a smuggler
to the eponymous hero may well make our mouths water
in these days of austerity. They began with Ostend oysters
en matelot; do these last words stand for 'en matelote'? If
so, am I wrong in thinking that *matelote* implies onions, and
that onions and oysters go ill together? Then there was a
small capon *truffé* and cutlets *aux pointes d'asperge,* which
call for no comment. The following paragraph concerning
the wines I quote, since it expresses a point of view about
Burgundy, which may perhaps be associated with the idea
mentioned above in connection with Horace Walpole that
Claret is the only wine improved by a sea voyage.

'A glass of Chablis with your oysters; what a pity those
Burgundy wines are inaccessible to you in England!
Chablis scarcely bears the sea—of half a dozen bottles one is
drinkable; the same of the red wines; and what is there so
generous?—not that we are to despise our old friend
Champagne. And now you've helped yourself to a pâté, let
us have a bumper. By the bye, have they abandoned that

127

absurd notion they used to have in England about Champagne? When I was there, they never served it after soup: your glass of Sherry or Madeira is a holocaust offered up to bad cookery; for if the soup were safe, Chablis or Sauternes is your fluid.'

Their supper ended with dessert and the drinking of red Burgundy, the host 'looking with ecstasy at the rich colour of the wine through the candle,' while he prepared himself for the telling of a story that called for the opening of another bottle.

The suggestion that neither red Burgundy nor Chablis —it is to be noted that Lever does not mention Montrachet or Meursault—could stand the journey across the Channel strikes a new note. No doubt in recent times the stamina of white wines has been greatly increased by improved methods of vinification. The careful dosage of sulphur used by the Germans for Hock and Moselle has augmented their powers of endurance and helped to preserve the wines crystal bright in defiance of the camouflage offered by the traditional coloured wine glass. Chablis again as a light white wine particularly subject to loss of transparency has no doubt profited by Pasteur's discoveries concerning fermentation, and can face the Channel crossing with equanimity. It does, however, seem surprising that Lever, who was unquestionably very interested in wine, should have raised doubts about red Burgundy.

His smuggler would presumably have been pleased by the unfortunate habit developed in late Victorian days of drinking Champagne throughout the meal, though he does seem to make a reservation in favour of Chablis or Sauternes.

Professor Saintsbury has set his hall-mark on Bishop, since he gives his recipe for the making of this mulled Port in *Notes on a Cellar-Book*, the addition of half an orange stuck full of cloves and the lighting of the vapour of the liquid as soon as it is warm. Lever tells us of the fatal effect of 'a bowl of smoking bishop, spiced and seasoned to perfection,' drunk at the Kursaal of Kreuznach after bumpers of Champagne, which sent a young man so fast asleep that he was at the mercy of a pack of card-sharpers, who swore next day that he owed them £700. Truly mulled Port on the top of Champagne would seem to be asking for trouble, since there appears to be some fundamental disharmony between Champagne and Port in its natural state.

Later in *Arthur O'Leary*, the Reuten-Krantz inn at Eisenach, provides the scene for a Gargantuan banquet provided unawares by mine host for a whole succession of the officers of the Chasseurs de la Garde during the retreat from Leipzig. We hear of a table groaning under good things 'amid which, like Lombardy poplars in a Flemish landscape, the tall and taper necks of various flasks shot up —some frosted with an icy crust, some cobwebbed with the touch of time.' The soup was accompanied by a glass of 'Nieder-thaler'—'no hock was ever like it'—the description, alas! is inadequate for the identification of this incomparable Hock of unknown vintage. Then there came a *pâté en béchamel* with a glass of Chablis mine host could vouch for. 'Such a glass of wine might console the Emperor for Leipzig.' If Lever had said Montrachet, we might have believed him; for Montrachet might have stood up against the incomparable Hock, but the poor little delicate Chablis, however fine its quality, cannot have had a chance on the palate after any Rhine wine worthy of such commendation.

There followed trout fried in mushroom gravy, and dashed with anchovy—I must admit that this dish sounds to me rather like a contradiction in terms—and up goes a cry for Œil de Perdrix, that partridge-eye Champagne which in Saintsbury's judgment almost deserves the epithet poetic on the pattern of pheasant-eye narcissus. I feel some slight doubt as to the exact hue of the partridge's eye, rather suspecting that it possessed a tinge of pink, but Larousse defines it as 'paillet, vif et brillant,' so that straw colour would seen to be its prevailing shade. At any rate we learn that the Œil de Perdrix of the *Rue-Garland* consisted of Ay Mousseux, a reminder of the good old days when Cham-

129   I

pagne was not yet known by the names of famous firms.
Then we may suppose blending of the various strains of
wine from black grape and white on which modern Champagne depends was still in its infancy, and Ay must have
won the reputation that it has preserved to this day of being
the one Champagne district which can produce wines worthy
of the best of all sparkling wines without admixture of wines
from any other district. After many bumpers and many
flasks of the Ay Mousseux, there followed Hock, Hermitage
and Bordeaux unspecified as to their more particular origin,
and with the dessert a glass of mulled Claret with cloves.

Lever's O'Leary, while hunting the fox on the banks of
the Meuse, was run away with by an ill-conditioned roan,
and is followed in his wild career by the lovely Laura, who
eventually finds herself in the compromising situation of
being alone with him in the inn of a village, from which
they cannot possibly return home before nightfall. We are
not concerned with the Irishman's narrow escape from a sort
of Gretna Green match known as *mariage sous la cheminée*
with a runaway beauty, but it is pleasant to find that their
tête-à-tête dinner was washed down by Haut Brion of
excellent, though of unnamed, vintage. Almost one is
prepared for the young man claiming the premier *cru* of
Graves as Irish wine after the fashion of Maurice Healy,
insisting that its patronymic clearly is derived from the Isle
of Saints, but Lever enters into no verbal niceties about
Château O'Brien. Finally, I observe that he describes
Rosenthaler, a *wine to kiss*, as Goethe's favourite Rhenish.
If, as he says, Goethe had a good taste in wine, we should
have been glad of further particulars, for Rosenthaler
remains more than vague. No one, however, can question
the truth of the following dictum. 'You great folk ever like
to show some decided preference to one vintage above the
rest. Napoleon adopted Chambertin, Joseph the Second
drank nothing but Tokay, and Peter the Great found
Brandy the only fluid to his palate.'

PART THREE

Wine Yesterday and Today:
Science, Sherry
and Austerity

I

Pasteur and the Wine-Grower

I T seems reasonable to date from Pasteur's discovery of the principles of fermentation the modern epoch in the history of wine, though the practical influence of scientific knowledge on the quality of great wine has proved to be almost negligible. In 1864, after six years of investigation, Pasteur was able to announce that he had solved the mystery which had puzzled mankind, ever since *Noah began to be a husbandman and planted a vineyard and drank of the wine and was drunken,* just 4,211 years before if we accept the delightfully definite chronology of the Bible margin. It was natural to suppose that his success would revolutionize the time-honoured traditions of wine-making and make good wine a more familiar creature than it had ever been. The revelation that the work of fermenting grape juice was carried out by living organisms lurking in the bloom of the fruit came as a surprise to those who had seen in it no more than a chemical process, though it confirmed the more romantic view of those who held that wine was not only a symbol of life, but actually a living thing. It was hoped that human skill and knowledge would now be able to condition the conversion of grape juice into wine, so that grower and producer would be independent of the caprices of weather and geography. The finest wine would be mass-

133

produced, as if its nature were no higher than that of artificial silk or cash registers.

Science would destroy the inferior bacteria of grapes grown in inferior soil and climate and replace them with microbes grown in famous wine districts, so that the sourest ordinary would be converted into glorious Claret or Burgundy. Wines were to be aged in a few weeks instead of maturing for years. 'For the consumer,' said M. Malvezin, of Haut-Bailly, 'a château of high rank should always be a great wine. . . . It should have every year the same alcoholic strength, the same breed, the same bouquet, thanks to the work of our scientists with the immortal Pasteur at their head.' In fact, there was no end to the miracles that were to be worked. No wonder Pasteur in 1865 took out patents not only for the pasteurization of wine—'the raising of the temperature of newly-made wine to a degree sufficient to kill or render definitely inactive the ferments and germs it may contain,' to quote M. André Simon's *Encyclopaedia of Gastronomy*—but also for the artificial ageing of the imitation wines made in the Midi.

Very partial has been the fulfilment of all these bright hopes. M. Malvezin applied all the science of Pasteur to his Haut-Bailly of 1918, but I have yet to hear that Haut-Bailly, 1918, was an historic wine, or indeed a wine of any outstanding merit. Unsound wines have been saved again and again by pasteurization, but when it is applied to wines of high repute, it proves that there is something wrong with them. The case of Lafite 1928 is not yet forgotten. Ironically enough all the good that Pasteur's research seemed likely to achieve was completely wiped out by phylloxera, the pest that preys on vine roots and was brought from the New World as well as those other scourges of the wine-grower; oidium, mildew and black rot. Never again in our time were there to be such wines as the succession of great Clarets grown between 1864 and 1878. The best that science could do was to provide palliatives for a plague which demolished the vine plants from the root upwards.

Some twenty years ago, the Empire Marketing Board sent Professor Hewitt to France, Germany, and Algiers to produce a Report on the Chemistry of Wine-Making for the benefit of Dominion wine-growers, and all his efforts resulted in very little more than an investigation of the causes of the wine disease called *casse*, which he found to be due to the presence of minute quantities of iron in the liquid, confirming the traditional custom of allowing no metal other than silver or bronze to touch the must. His chief conclusion was that the property of wine which the French call *moelleux*, or *velouté* depends on the presence of fruit jelly, and that this is partly responsible for the rich velvety texture of the great Sauternes. The pectin content is increased by the heating of the must and more particularly by the over-ripening of the grapes which encourages the 'noble mould,' both in Sauternes and on the Rhine. The Professor hoped that the newly-acquired knowledge of pectin compounds would make it possible to obtain this very desirable quality in all high-grade wines and also to raise wines from a lower class into a higher. He told me of these laudable aspirations one night at the Savage Club, and, thinking that enough time had now elapsed since 1928 for some signs of accomplishment, I turned hopefully to the Wine Section of the *Encyclopaedia of Gastronomy*, confident that if pectin was really all it was set up to be, I should find a reference to its influence on modern wines. Alas! pectin is not mentioned, and I'm very much afraid that no wine of quality ever yet owed any *moelleux* at all to the artificial introduction of this jelly-producing substance.

The Professor, it must be said, set out the reasons why science fails when it tries to analyse the essence of wine, its bouquet and aroma, and is comparatively powerless in its dealings with its subtlest qualities. There are too many imponderables to be weighed up. 'When consideration,' he writes, 'is given to the substances which produce the essentially vinous flavour, difficulty is experienced.' After some alarming chemical formula concerning esters and acetals, he touches on amino-acids, aldehydes, tannin and pectin, and winds up with a confession of failure. 'But when the flavour due to all the above causes has been dealt with as well as the possible presence of small amounts of oils extracted from the seeds, there still remains a bouquet peculiar to an individual wine which cannot be expressed in terms of any of the afore-mentioned substances. Odoriferous substances occur in the skins of grapes and, concerning their composition, practically nothing is known.' In fact the chemical analysis of a great wine omits the one interesting point—in virtue of what substance does it differ from an ordinary wine.

The consequences of Pasteur's great discovery have been disappointing for the lover of fine wines, since, eighty years after, we have had no succession of great vintages such as that which ended in 1878. Nature seems to have been aggrieved by the divulgation of her secrets, and refused us that series of good years without which the vineyards cannot attain their best. The Champagne growers at any rate owe science a debt; for the saccharometer has made it possible to gauge exactly the amount of sugar responsible for the sparkle and therefore the pressure that will be exercised on the walls of the bottle, while in the past the rough-and-ready judgment of taste often resulted in a disastrous percentage of breakages due to the bottles exploding under the pressure of carbonic gas. It has long been hoped that the scientists would succeed in exposing the cause of 'corking' in wine, that fungus taste which comes so unaccountably from the cork; but all research has proved fruitless, and it is still doubtful whether the trouble is to be ascribed to some filter-passing microbe or something materially wrong with the cork.

Before this last war the German wine-growers were

undoubtedly far in advance of their European competitors in the application of scientific methods to wine production. Sulphur has been the great wine antiseptic since Roman times, and casks are still purified by the burning of a sulphur match inside them—just as Cato did in his day. White wines need sulphur to keep them bright, and the Germans used a sulphurous acid bomb which made it possible to measure the dose given with the utmost exactitude. More important, however, is the remarkable advance made in the use of filters to control and stop fermentation. It is claimed that wines may be passed through so fine a filter that all the yeasts and germs, good or bad, are removed without injuring the quality of the wines. All organisms are supposed to be held up by its series of films, and all substances that give it bouquet and aroma to pass through them unimpaired. In a word, the filter performs by percolation what pasteurization accomplishes by heat. It is probable that the filter will never be available for red wines, since colouring matter would hardly be able to find a way through such exiguous meshes. Of course, once the wine has been filtered, it is dead so far as vinous life is concerned, and age can only bring decay. On the other hand, there is no danger of the filter causing that *goût du cuit* which is one of the charges brought against pasteurized wine. It enables the fermentation of wine to be arrested, when it still contains sugar that would otherwise go to the composition of alcohol, and so it makes it possible to dispense with the addition of sugar in the case of wines which in the old days would have to be 'improved' when fermented out. The filter is certainly not a device desirable for the finest wines, since it eliminates their slow and natural development, but for the average beverage wine which was in the past artificially sweetened, it can claim consideration, since everyone who respects wine will agree that it is safer to take from it than to add to it.

Pasteur tells us that it was on the special request of the Emperor Napoleon III that he undertook, in 1863, his

137

researches into the diseases of wine, which completed his inquiry into alcoholic fermentation and prepared the way for his discoveries of the part played by germs in the infectious diseases of mankind. André Simon gave me the volume of the *Works of Pasteur* containing his account of these researches, just when I was puzzling my brain over the second fermentation to which the peculiar character of a Fino Sherry was attributed, and to my delight and surprise I found in this book an answer to the problem. Pasteur, as a native of Arbois, had carried out his experiments with Jura wine, and no one had thought of connecting the exceptional·behaviour of these wines, for which he had found the explanation, with the similar eccentricity of Sherry.

I had been present at the Sherry vintage, and seen the wines of Jerez undergoing the treatment which produces the unique Fino taste and bouquet, a treatment which in any other wine district would be regarded as inexcusable neglect; for it consists in leaving butts of maturing young wines in the most unlikely places; on a garden path, for instance, the casks being on ullage and apparently exposed to the attacks of every enemy of good wine. Yet the excellence of the process is proved by the excellence and hardy constitution of the wine so produced. After reading Pasteur, I made up my mind that I would take my next holiday in the Jura and see for myself, on the spot, the wines with which he had experimented.

The essence of his discovery was this: if wines are left exposed to the air, they will soon be thickly covered by a layer or film called a *mycoderma*, composed of 'flower,' or micro-organisms, and his experiments showed that there were two forms of this *mycoderma* sufficiently like one another to deserve the names of Tweedledum and Tweedledee, though they were quite different in their nature and their effect on the wine. One of these was the *mycoderma aceti*, the vinegar microbe, the other the *mycoderma vini,* which exercises its influence in the wines of the Jura and of Jerez. These mycodermas appear on the surface of all fermented liquids, and there is a 'flower' of beer and cider as well as of wine and vinegar. The Romans knew of them, and they were not far out in thinking that the appearance of a clean white 'flower' is a sign of a good wine; for when the beneficent *mycoderma vini* holds the field, the 'flower' is a pure white, and when it is being overcome by the vinegar microbe it fades and takes the colour of the wine.

Before Pasteur, no one had any conception of the vital part played by the microscopically small in the economy of the world. As he says: 'If these microscopic beings disappeared from our globe, the surface of the earth would be piled high with dead organic matter and corpses of every kind, both animal and vegetable. They are mainly responsible for giving to oxygen its property of combustion. Without them life would become impossible, because the work of death would be incomplete.'

When Pasteur began his search for the microbe that turned wine into vinegar, he started by cultivating a mycoderma on some Arbois wine. His film of micro-organisms duly appeared after the wine had been left exposed to the air, but to his astonishment he was unable to detect any acetic acid as having been formed by the action of the 'flower' on the alcohol. True, the alcohol began to disappear, but not a trace of vinegar was to be found in its stead. He even added some acetic acid to the wine; it promptly vanished like the alcohol. It was clear that this 'flower' of the Arbois wine did not produce vinegar, but destroyed it. On the other hand, when the same experiment was made with another wine, Burgundy, for instance, as soon as the 'flower' was formed, the production of vinegar began. The Arbois 'flower,' *mycoderma vini*, took oxygen from the air and combined it with alcohol, taking eight or twelve molecules of oxygen to combine with one molecule of alcohol and converting the alcohol into water and carbonic acid, the final stage of combustion. The vinegar 'flower' seized on two to four molecules of oxygen and combined them with one of alcohol, to form acetic acid, which is, as it were, a half-way house on the road to combustion. The vinegar, of course, spells ruin to the wine. The *mycoderma vini*, on the other hand, causes no more than a loss of alcohol and the production of something neutral which does nothing worse than weaken the aroma and tend to flatness.

With these facts in my head, I set off to Arbois bent on trying the Jura wines and above all on making the acquaintance of the famous local wine, Château Châlon, which claimed a longevity that threw Dr. Middleton's Senatorial Port into the shade. When Millerand was President of the Republic in 1920, he was presented with specimens of Château Châlon 1811, the famous Comet Year, and 1774, both described as sound and agreeable to the palate.

I found Arbois a peculiarly charming little town. With its arcades and courtyards, it was singularly different from the average *ville de province*, and its inhabitants were remarkable for good looks and an open-handed generosity, which one does not usually associate with the French provinces. It seemed to me stamped with the hallmark of Spanish high-mindedness; for it is a town of Franche Comté, which had been under Spanish rule until 1768, when under Louis XIV it became part of France. I cannot help thinking that it must be more than a coincidence that the wines of this eastern province of France and those of the south of Spain should have so curious a feature in common. It may well be that vines brought from Spain, Spanish methods of vine-culture and wine-making have left their impression on the wines of Arbois and the neighbourhood.

Underground cellars are a rarity in French wine districts except in Champagne, but in the Jura the wine-grower's house generally stands on the top of a very ancient cellar, often very small but close packed with barrels. Wine-making is performed on that small scale which promises quality and distinction, and the pressing of the grapes and the maturing of the wine is a household affair. In the cellar of the Mayor of Ménétru, one of the communes that produce the Château Châlon wine, I was able to examine the *mycoderma vini* that formed a thick film on the surface of a cask containing a wine that had been there nearly twenty years. This film really serves the purpose of a cork, for it cuts off the wine below it from the air, and as the microbes that form it are excessively greedy for oxygen, they will not allow the smallest trace of it to reach the wine. Paradoxically, the Jura wine-grower, by exposing his wine to the atmosphere and allowing the *mycoderma vini* to form, deprives his wine of oxygen. The oxygen can only reach the wine in the form of water and carbonic acid after combination with the alcohol.

The 'flower' also protects the wine from the assaults of the vinegar microbe, which does from time to time show itself even in the Jura wines; for the two mycodermas are deadly foes and Pasteur gives a vivid account of the pitched battles watched under the microscope in which great armies of microbes were engaged on either side with varying result.

Pasteur had no doubt that the encouragement of the wine 'flower' on the Arbois wines was dictated by the nature of the grapes grown in the district. Though it did enfeeble certain qualities of wine and reduce the alcoholic strength, it was necessary for the development of the special characteristics by which those particular wines were distinguished. He connected the affinity of wines with one or other of the 'flowers' to the bouquet peculiar to the grapes from which they were made. The fruit of the great vines of Bordeaux, Burgundy, and the Rhine, the *pinot*, the *cabernet* and the *Riesling*, possesses an exquisite perfume, which it seems to

141

impart directly to the wine. The best grapes of the Jura, the *ploussard* and the *savagnin*, lack this bouquet, and the same may be said of the Sherry grapes. Pasteur believed that the *mycoderma vini* did not appear, as a rule, where the full beauty of bouquet existed, and that if it did, it would interfere with the production of the delicate volatile elements that form it, by the very efficacy with which it secludes the wine it covers from the air. Oxygen plays an important part in the formation of bouquet. On the other hand, the pleasant clean, nutty scent, which develops into an intensely subtle bouquet and distinguishes both Château Châlon and Sherry, appears to arise from oxidation after the *mycoderma vini* has prepared the way for combination. For this reason bottle age, when, with the wine separated from the 'flower,' this oxidation can take place, has great importance in the excellence of both these wines.

It would certainly appear that the predominance of wine 'flower' in the Jura wines is due to the character of the grapes, for all the wines of the district, red and white, ordinary and fine, are inclined to produce it. The ordinary wines which are only left with the 'flower' for a short time are pleasant enough as a beverage, but they are inclined to flabbiness, whenever the *ploussard* is mixed with the less distinguished but equally indigenous *trousseau*, and they suffer from a tendency to flatness which is to be observed even in the rarest and finest Château Châlon. At least that is my opinion. When one first comes across a wine which is out of the ordinary, one that most of one's friends have never tasted, one is tempted to exaggerate its merits and overlook its defects. Every goose becomes a swan, and one encourages one's fellows in the belief, *omne ignotum pro magnifico.* So I fear that in the enthusiasm of my first visits to Arbois I set the wine of Château Châlon on a higher plane than Bacchus would allow it in the ordering of his vintages and growths. Maybe I was influenced by Morton Shand who wrote so eloquently about Château

142

Châlon as 'one of the great and classical wines of France,' and its 'peculiar nasturtium leaf flavour that is sometimes encountered in very old and dry Sherry.' I believe my exploration of the Jura encouraged Walter Berry to extend his journey, *In Search of Wine*, to Arbois, and he waxed as enthusiastic as I did over the twin brother of Château Châlon known as Château d'Arlay. Of Château d'Arlay 1928, he said, 'when you taste it for the first time, you will be nonplussed. First, you will say, Sherry—then, perhaps, Marsala; then, no, it is like a cross between the two. But it is entirely a species of its own.' 'Certainly these wines of Château d'Arlay are remarkable; there is nothing in the world to compare with them.'

How I wish I could discuss them now after all these years with Walter! I am sure he would disagree with me, but none the less I am pretty certain that underneath he would have a sneaking sympathy with the point of view that these esoteric wines, which rarely go outside their own locality, are very fine wines—for a small wine party. Taken by themselves in the seclusion of their homes, where there is no competition to raise fine points of excellence, they deserve all the superlatives we can shower upon them, but when they are brought out into the wide world and are faced by wines whose names and virtues are household words, they have to take a second, if honourable, place. They are rather curiosities than masterpieces of the wine-grower's art.

There is one thing that I have noticed in tasting the finest examples of Château Châlon and even the champion Château d'Arlay 1928—there is something lacking, something that falls short of the standard that one sets up for a really great wine. It may be that now I am prejudiced by the thought that all those years spent with *mycoderma vini* turning alcohol and oxygen into water must have had a prejudicial effect on the wine. At any rate I seem to detect a suspicion of flatness, almost mawkishness, where there should be the stimulus of freshness. No such reproach can be brought against Sherry, but in Sherry any tendency to dull neutrality is corrected by the added wine spirit. The unfortified *vin jaune*, to use the special name of these Jura wines, just lacks the fillip that is so delightful in the lightest and dryest of Finos.

Pasteur's experiments were in no way connected with the curious vicissitudes during the last century or so in the history of the wine shipped to this country from the Jerez district of Spain. In the early nineteenth century the only Sherry known in this country belonged to the class of rich dessert wine such as we now distinguish as Oloroso. Those light, dry wines, which are so much appreciated, were known only in Spain, and much prejudice had to be overcome before they were accepted for what they are—the best *apéritif* in the world.

One of the earliest records of that austere wine Manzanilla to be found in English appears in the Journal of a certain Mr. James Busby, who came from New South Wales to study the production of Sherry and, after a three weeks' journey from London, reached Jerez-de-la-Frontera in the year of grace, 1831. 'We stopped at a *venta* or public-house,' he writes, 'to obtain a glass of the wine called Manzanilla, the *vin du pays* of the district, which Dr. Wilson assures me is preferred to all other wines by people of all ranks in the country; it is unknown in the cellars of the English merchants, but is a light, pleasant beverage, having at the same time a mellowness and flavour, which I have no doubt would, after a little habit, procure for it preference even with those who would find it insipid at the first trial.'

Some thirty years later, before Manzanilla and Fino had made their appearance on the Victorian sideboard, my father, who was in the Navy, paid a visit to Cádiz and Jerez, and there he made acquaintance with the clean, dry nuttiness of Manzanilla, and fell a victim to its charm.

Ever afterwards, wherever he might be stationed, he contrived to maintain a modest supply of a wine that appealed to him as the dryest of the dry, and when he retired there was always a glass of Manzanilla and a biscuit for any chance caller. By that time the English wine merchant had added both Manzanillas and Finos to his catalogue, and though the popularity of Sherry suffered for a time most unfortunately from a spate of imitation and low quality wines not worthy of the name, he never failed to have a few bottles of first-rate Manzanilla in the cellar, claiming for himself a certain amount of credit in having discerned its virtues before it became generally known to the public.

The story of dry Sherry and its rise to popularity in these islands forms one of the oddest chapters in the annals of wine. The Finos and other dry, light wines owe to the 'flower,' the *mycoderma vini*, their unique attraction as an *apéritif* and that distinctive delicacy and austerity of flavour which cleanses the palate as no other wine is capable of doing. In the earlier days of the Sherry trade, wines were not encouraged to 'flower' and those that did so heavily were regarded as spoilt for the English market and not worth exporting. They were disposed of at a low price for local consumption and that was how Mr. Busby was able to obtain as a great novelty a glass of Manzanilla at a wayside inn in 1831. It was not until the 'sixties that the possibility of these wines appealing to the English taste occurred to the shippers of Jerez. In *Old Sherry*, the history of 'the first hundred years of Gonzalez, Byass and Co.,' we find the following reference to the introduction of dry Sherry in England. 'The popularity of the Fino and lighter types of Amontillado Sherries in certain parts of Spain resulted in a daring suggestion on the part of the young Byasses that they should be introduced to the English market. Since, at this comparatively recent date, all Sherry wine sent to England was still of the Oloroso type, what they suggested was a very bold experiment indeed, and one that would undoubtedly revolutionize the whole business for better or worse. In the early 'seventies customers of English wine merchants were asked to taste for the first time a "very dry" Sherry (nowadays hardly considered "dry" at all) shipped by Gonzalez, Byass and Co., under the name of "Vino de Pasto".'

Such a bold innovation inevitably met with the opposition of those who had formed an idea of Sherry as a rich, dessert wine, and simply could not think of it as anything else. It is a human failing, and I confess that the miraculous beauty of the famous Berncastler Doctor Trocken-beeren Auslese of 1921 came to me with a sense of impropriety; Moselles had no right to be so extravagantly wonderful. Mr. Tovey, who wrote *Wine and Wine Countries*, first edition 1861, second edition 1877, has no good word for Manzanilla, and tells the story of an Earl of Derby who, suffering from gout, was sent by his wine merchant a bottle of Manzanilla as a sample with the assurance that it would eradicate the disorder. His lordship merely replied that he preferred the gout.

Tovey makes no attempt to conceal his horror at the breeding of 'flower,' when he witnessed it in Spain. Indeed, he regarded it with the same disgust as that which a vague rumour about pasteurization as a means of ageing wine had aroused in his conservative breast. He was surprised that little or no care was taken to exclude the external air from the casks, still more astonished to find that they were wanting fourteen or sixteen gallons of being full and, finally, dumbfounded to perceive 'floating upon the surface of the wine something I can only compare to small native oysters taking a swim without their shells, but which I knew at once was fungus, showing more or less a progress towards decay.' Later, he concludes: 'Whoever first introduced this breeding of Fino ought to be subject to an *auto-da-fé*, for he has done more injury to the Sherry trade . . . than will be recovered in the present century.'

Yet if Mr. Tovey, who quotes Homer on his title page, had consulted his Pliny, he would have discovered that the ancient Romans did not share his abhorrence for the *mycoderma vini*. Pasteur observed that if the wine flower predominated over the vinegar microbe it was of a white, velvety colour, while if it was in danger of being overcome, it faded and took on the colour of the wine. So Pliny tells us that the wine 'flower' is a good sign, if it is white and clean in appearance. How amazed Mr. Tovey would be today to find that Sherry had become almost the synonym of a dry wine and that one of the hardships brought upon us by the war which was most resented was the deprivation of those light, dry wines which he despised!

[P.S. When the foregoing pages were already in type, the writer visiting Jerez learnt from Sr. Bobadilla, the head of the Wine Institute there, that the 'flower' is no longer ranked as a *mycoderma*, but as a *saccharomyces*, a phase of the principal agent of vinous fermentation *saccharomyces cerevisiae ellipsoideus*. Under this alias the yeast pursues the same activities in the same manner as Pasteur describes.]

Sherry in Fiction and the Edwardian Auction Room

M Y good friend E. C. Bentley, the sole begetter of that rival to the Limerick, the Clerihew, and the author of *Trent's Last Case*, appended to the notes on Sherry I had derived from Pasteur the following notions about that wine which he owed to Edgar Allan Poe. He had been reading *The Cask of Amontillado*, which happens not to be in my collection of Poe's tales, and what he read there about wine had tickled his fancy. The scene is laid in Rome *during the supreme madness of the carnival season* in a period when people wore *roquelaures* and popped on silk masks from time to time. Fortunato, with whose cruel fate the story deals, *prided himself on his connoisseurship in wine*, and the teller of the story, Montresor, claims to be equally gifted in this respect. 'I was skilful in the Italian vintages myself, and bought largely whenever I could.'

One day Montresor, plotting murder against Fortunato, confides in his future victim the startling news: 'I have received a pipe of what passes for Amontillado, and I have my doubts.' 'How!' exclaims Fortunato. 'Amontillado? A pipe? Impossible!' On first thoughts I credited Poe with the elementary technical knowledge that the pipe is the home of Port and the butt, the home of Sherry, but the solecism

148

passes unnoticed even by Fortunato's connoisseurship.
What was agitating him was the idea that Amontillado
was a rarity of rarities and as unlikely to be found in bulk
as Tokay Essence. Montresor says that he is on his way to
find his friend Luchesi and ask him what he thinks of the
wine.

'Luchesi,' replies Fortunato crushingly, 'is quite incapable of telling Amontillado from Sherry.'

And later tells Montresor what he thinks about Amontillado. 'Amontillado! You have been imposed upon; and as for
Luchesi, he cannot distinguish Sherry from Amontillado.'

One wonders whether he could have distinguished Saint
Emilion or Médoc from Claret. It is sad Poe could not have
referred to André Simon's wine *Encyclopaedia*, where he
would have read: 'Amontillado, one of the most popular
types of Sherry, neither too dry nor too sweet. It may be a
Fino or merely a *Vino de Pasto* wine in quality, but it is
meant to possess a fairly dry finish, somewhat similar to
the finish of the wines of Montilla near Cordoba.' Poe
might try to excuse himself with the plea that he was con-
fusing Amontillado with Montilla, which is not a Jerez
wine at all, though within it under another name there
flourishes the austerely generous spirit of Sherry, but
Montresor does nothing to restore his creator's reputation
for connoisseurship. Taking Fortunato to view this remarkable pipe, he draws a bottle from a mouldering pile, knocks
off its neck and announces that 'a draught of this Médoc
will defend us from the damps.' This summary method of
decanting, when apparently there was no trouble with the
cork, and the denial of Sherry-hood to Amontillado, reduce
Poe as a connoisseur of wine to the level of the lady novelist
who opined that Cheval Blanc must be a white wine,
though she probably did not expect Black and White
Whisky to be striped. At any rate, Fortunato is left, walled
up alive in the cellar to reflect, till death releases him, on the
distinction between Sherry and Amontillado.

Later, I thought that Poe's ideas about Sherry might be derived from the wine-merchants' price lists of his day. It would be surprising if the American wine merchant were any more precise and accurate than his opposite number in this country, and it would not be difficult to account for the discrimination between Sherry and Amontillado by the entries on the undated price list of a London firm, which from internal evidence must belong to the early 'seventies, when Sherry had attained the zenith of its popularity in this country. It opens with the offer of Sherries, undescribed as to character though varying in price; then under separate headings come Amontillado, Manzanilla, Amoroso, Montilla, Pajarete, as though they had no claim to the title of Jerez wines, as obviously the last two have not, and the list ends with Rota Tent, that Spanish red sacramental wine, which I learn from a ledger entry was purchased by King Edward VII to the amount of twelve dozen, though speculation as to what His Majesty may have done with it stimulates the imagination. So great was the vogue of Sherry at this time that more varieties of the Spanish wines we include in this category find a place in the catalogue than those of any other wine, Port, Claret, and Champagne offering a far more limited choice.

Just about this time Ouida was writing in a frenzy of seriousness her extravaganza of what the French call *le high life* in *Under Two Flags*, and from time to time in its pages Sherry makes a dignified appearance, once or twice as a Sherry-cobbler or a Sherry-peg, but usually with the honourable appellation of Regency, less pretentious perhaps than the vague Napoleon so light-heartedly attached to Brandies of doubtful lineage, and presumably referring to the oft-recurring 1820 Solera. Ouida's novel was first published in a military periodical in 1867, and heaven only knows what 'the swells in the Guards,' as she calls them, thought of her Heliogabalian description of their sybaritic existence. Regency Sherry flourishes on the hunting-field lodged in the most expensive of gold flasks—does not one of her Guardsmen stir the fire with the solid gold poker?—and assumes a startling role in justification of Tennyson's

> after-dinner talk
> Across the walnuts and the wine.

A hard-bitten peer, whom 'the Punjab knew as the Sword of the Evil One,' in the intervals between draughts of Hock, dropped walnuts into his Regency Sherry after the fashion of olives in a cocktail; unfortunately we are not told whether he gulped them down with the noble wine or fished them out before he tossed off the bumper.

After the 'seventies, Sherry was, like Lucifer, cast down from its high estate, its glory obscured by a cloud of fakes and imitations from the wine factories of Hamburg, and probably reached its nadir in 1901, when Edward VII, on his accession to the throne, sold 5,000 dozen of Sherry from the royal cellars by auction. One wonders what Queen Victoria would have thought of this commercial adventure on her son's part, which created a terrific sensation and brought in £18,000. The newspapers of the day were full of speculations and comments about this precedent. What, they wondered, were the chances that His Majesty would next indulge in a sale of surplus furniture and works of art? It was suggested that there were things in the royal palaces which might be disposed of without more serious loss to their possessors than the possibly unwanted Sherry in the cellars. One or two irreverent writers hinted that it was His Majesty's liver which was responsible for this wholesale disposal of his Sherry. Officially, however, it was explained that Sherry had gone out of fashion, was indeed an obsolete wine, and that the royal cellars contained a stock that would have lasted a hundred years at the actual rate of consumption. Leading articles attributed its downfall to the influence of the physician, who apparently in those days went nap on

Hock, Champagne, and Port as really wholesome wines, and hinted darkly at hepatic affections resulting from an indulgence in the wine of Jerez, and one writer boldly declared that the modern palate had become incapable of discriminating between Sherry and Madeira; I admit to doubts as to whether the scribe had tasted either.

A West End restaurant-keeper was interviewed and had no hesitation about hitting a wine when it was down; for he told the reporter that he knew at once who the customer would be when he heard that someone had asked for Sherry. It was certain to be an old-fashioned lady up from the provinces to shop. She would want half a bottle of Sherry with her lunch, because she was horrified at the raffish immorality of such up-to-date wines as Hock and Champagne. The dear Queen had not drunk such wines. It is to be observed that she wanted Sherry to drink with her meal: so Vino de Pasto would probably have been her demand. Today, though most people know that Sherry is a wine of all work, there are very few who would be inclined to drink Sherry while they ate. Saintsbury recommended the practice of drinking Manzanilla and the lightest Sherries in large tall beakers like old-fashioned beer-glasses, saying that they provided a real beverage which 'goes with anything from oysters . . . to anything short of sweets.' He also found that 'the medium Sherries—neither quite austere nor quite luscious— . . . may be taken to utmost satisfaction with food or without it, at any time in the day, except the first thing in the morning and the last at night.' The King's Sherries were nearly all of them of the rich after-dinner variety, though there were some lots of Amontillado, and their sale betokened not so much the decline of Sherry in popular favour as the transition period between its renown as an after-dinner wine and its return to grace as an *apéritif*.

Admittedly the worst moments of the guest at the solemn Victorian dinner were spent in the drawing room, when the party was waiting for their meal and the arrival of their most important member, who was stressing his value by coming late. There was no refreshment to while away the time and nothing to start the flow of conversation in a society in which, unlike the French, artificial stimulation was needed before any exchange of ideas apart from spasmodic remarks about the weather could take place. The reader need not be reminded of *Crotchet Castle* and the dismal account of the melancholy period that preceded the serving of a ceremonial meal. Tongue-tied incompetence in the social art of light conversation was largely responsible for the universal vogue of Champagne in the 'nineties with its instantaneous unloosening of the bonds of shyness and silence, and to this failing must be ascribed the eager reception of the American cocktail only tempered into civilization by the introduction of the light, dry Sherry which is the perfect prelude to a good wine.

At first sight the sale of the royal Sherries would seem to have been the final confirmation of the bankruptcy of the Spanish wine, but great is the influence of the snobbish instinct. High prices were given for them—some pale golden wines fetched over 550s. a dozen—but the merchants who purchased them did not lose on their investment, and the way was prepared for the popular welcome given in the later years of the century to the Amontillados, Finos, and Manzanillas, with which the name of Sherry is now generally connected. Saintsbury's menu for a Sherry dinner was arranged as follows: Manzanilla with oysters, Amontillado with entrées and roast, Amoroso with sweets, and for after dinner the oldest and brownest of *old browns*, say Brown Bristol Milk.

To return to some of Ouida's odd notions about drinks as expressed in *Under Two Flags*, we find her Guardsman hero, whose good looks were so admired by his fellow officers that they nicknamed him Beauty, drinking Curaçoa with his breakfast and apparently revelling in its sticky sweetness, though in the hectic life he led there can scarcely have been a single morning which was not the morning after. He was helped in the downward path of his extravagance and luxury by a young lady of French extraction known as Zu-Zu, a *coryphée*, we are told, whom he had 'translated from a sphere of garret, bread and cheese to a sphere of villa, Champagne, and chicken,' to grow immediately intolerant of any wine costing less than 90s. the dozen. How easy was the primrose path in those days! How cheap Swinburne's 'raptures and roses'! The spendthrift could go to the devil on Champagne no dearer than the Algerian of the poor and virtuous of today. It is really surprising that Zu-Zu kept her good looks; for we hear that she was a vulgar little soul with a catholic taste in drinks, 'drinking everything from Bass's ale to Rum punch, and from Cherry Brandy to Absinthe . . . and was as jolly as a grig, according to her own phraseology, so long as she could stew her pigeon in Champagne, and drink wines and liqueurs beyond price,' that is presumably sold at not less than 90s. the dozen. For Bertie the Beauty in moments of depression, at three in the morning, she prescribed Crême de Bouzy (whatever that may be) and Parfait Amour—a liqueur of violet hue which according to André Simon's *Concise Encyclopaedia* probably owes its renown to some elderly spinster who knew no better—in conjunction with pineapple ice. When, and how, she learnt to ride remains a mystery, but, following the hounds, she was only surpassed by that queen and huntress, unchaste and fair, the aristocratic Lady Guenevere, who after a marvellous run 'refused to dismount, but consented to take a biscuit and a little Lafitte [sic],' while that connoisseur Bertie, I regret to say, regaled himself with 'a deep draught of sparkling Rhenish.' Sparkling Hock has never seemed to me a refreshing or agreeable drink, either on or off the hunting field, but it was at least more tempting than a Champagne I found offered in a wine merchant's catalogue, dated 1882: Good Templar Champagne at half a crown a bottle guaranteed to contain not more than 9 per cent of alcohol.

Bertie, ruined and disgraced, enlists in the Foreign Legion and a lovely *vivandière*, Cigarette, falls in love with him. She is a remarkable girl; for she provides the troops with vintage Clarets and Burgundies, all casually blended in the little barrel she carries as the mark of her profession. Walter Berry says in *Viviana*, I know not on what authority, that this barrel was called a *cuppetin* and that from this word is derived the English tappit-hen, which stands for a large bottle in Walter Scott, and has come to mean a three bottle Magnum. I would beg my readers to avoid the horrible word Trignum, formed from Magnum, as though *Ma* was the Latin for *two* and *Gnum* for *bottles*. Cigarette, anyhow, fills up her tappit-hen at a party that is being given by the wicked Colonel of the regiment in an atmosphere reeking with tobacco smoke and heavy perfumes. The Clarets that are standing about in ice-pails must have possessed a terrific bouquet, since it succeeded in asserting itself through scent and nicotine, and Cigarette is careful to choose only the very best for the rank and file who were her customers.

It is noticeable that throughout the book the characters drink *soda and brandy* and not *brandy and soda*. Badminton is a favourite summer drink, a mild form of Claret Cup, if I can trust the *Concise Oxford Dictionary*, and someone gets drunk on Perles du Rhin, a beverage that remains unexplained. Villains drink 'Brandy-heated Roussillon,' which is apparently very expensive, and Moselle Cup is fashionable. In Ouida's world, Moselle is an odd sort of wine; for in another romance, *Chandos*, we hear of the 'tasteful foam of sparkling Moselle,' suggestive of malt liquor rather than the juice of the grape. Here a man may breakfast on Curaçoa and *pâté de foie gras*, though it is regarded as very French to combine peaches, grapes, chocolate, and Claret! An obscure epigram assures us that friendship is never sealed so firmly as with the green wax of a pure Claret, and the villain, while he is watching a game of baccarat, takes alternately glasses of Moselle and Maraschino, not perhaps without confusion to his internal economy. Even more eccentric is the hero who lifts to his lips 'a deep glass of glowing-red Roussillon,' while a lovely lady is crowning him with 'a wreath of crimson roses washed in purple Burgundy'; surely he would have been better advised to have drunk the Burgundy and reserved the glowing-red Roussillon for the washing of the roses. As it was he shook the wine from the rose-crown as he bent and kissed the glowing, Southern loveliness of Flora de l'Orme, the magnificent Arlésienne, who had twisted the wreath in the bright masses of his golden hair. I fear Chandos of Clarencieux, to give our Guardsman his full name, needed a lesson from André Simon as well as a hair-cut.

III

The Beverage of Austerity

ALAS! no meditation on wine under the heading of Yesterday and Today can overlook the compulsion of austerity which World War on World War has imposed on the wine-lover in a land that grows no wine. Its exigencies cannot but fill with lamentation many more pages than he needs for exultation over the slender benefits bestowed on him by modern science. So long as a man is unable to stand himself and his friends a bottle of wine without a feeling of prodigal extravagance, so long will what Chesterton called the Curse of Water lie heavy upon us, and the writer's fancy will be forced to stray, not among the springs and founts of Helicon, which inspire the poet's imagination with celestial wine, but among the prosaic wells, reservoirs, and taps which provide the drink of austerity, the water of affliction. I have never forgiven Pindar for opening his *Olympian Odes* with the challenging statement that water is superlatively best. As examples of absolutely first-class excellence he picks out water, gold which shines like fire on a dark night, the warmth of the sun, and the Olympian games. This preference for water annoyed me as a schoolboy and the more, as I grew older, I found myself entangled in the lyric poet's obscurities, the more I disliked his display of the blue ribbon.

Perhaps that is one of the reasons why in my house the praiseworthy wants of a very occasional water-drinking visitor are regularly forgotten. No choice of vintages from the tap or spring can I offer to my guests, though I depend on a shallow well, which produces tolerable drinking water as water goes. It is just like the stuff, that it is least unpalatable to drink when it is most unwholesome. At least I am assured that water from the chalk has a freshness and bloom upon it forbidden to water of other provenance, and doctors scream for filters and the kettle, when there is a hint of chalky sediment to prognosticate that bugbear of our forefathers, the stone. The gullible townsman cultivates a superstition that it is in the nature of water to run in pipes and gush out of taps, and I have had visitors aghast at the idea that my water comes out of a well before it reaches any cistern. The primitive method of water supply has its advantages and disadvantages. At least one is sure that no chemist has been monkeying with it and lending to it that taste of chlorine, which is now regarded by the town-dweller as its natural aroma. Years ago every summer Paris used to revel in water of more than vinous body and such a *terroir* tang as never vine produced. Whenever there was a drought, for some unexplained reason, the sewers and the water-mains entered into a conspiracy of amalgamation, and typhoid was only avoided by enormous doses of *eau de Javel*, until the water reeked worse than the drains. However, one did not drink Paris water; quite tolerable ordinary wine cost less than a franc a litre, and one washed one's teeth in Eau St. Galmier, a mineral water that came from an inexhaustible spring and was usually called by the unsophisticated peasant *eau pourrie*. The French countryman was as surprised to see water coming out of a bottle instead of wine as the Cockney of today at having to pump water from a well. Some years ago I had a cottage near Gatwick with a well that served in summer as a perfect refrigerator. A couple of bottles of white wine lowered into its depths would be drawn up with the freshness of an ideal temperature, and I remember that my cooling system once gained the approval of André Simon.

Restrictions are often imposed on those who depend on the automatic profusion of water-works, when the man with a good well knows no stint, though I must confess that of recent years I have had regularly to take precautions against drought, which would have seemed fantastic in my youth. The whole country has become wildly extravagant with the fluid once so lavishly supplied by Nature in these islands and she resents the abuse of her gifts. In this year of grace, 1950, she has manifested her indignation by the violence with which she has given us too much of that good thing, rain, and next year no doubt she will be as stingy as ever. Once the idea of a drought in these islands seemed a contradiction in terms; our trouble was incessant and excessive downpours, which made every Englishman instinctively sympathize with Noah. During the past thirteen years, there have been no less than seven droughts in the part of Berkshire in which I live and scarcely a year of average rainfall. It is admittedly an exceptionally dry belt, but our scarcity of rain over so long a period would have appeared ridiculous to the last generation.

My own well has resisted gallantly for all its shallowness; it is less than eighteen feet deep. In dry weather I can pump it very nearly dry to fill the five-hundred-gallon cistern, but in an hour or two it has filled again. The electric pump has had its failures, and though the contradictoriness of material objects makes it generally go wrong at week-ends, its faults have been corrected with surprising promptitude by the local blacksmith. Now my ancient well is to be superseded by a main supply, which is gradually creeping along the village lanes and which will most certainly be a blessing for those many cottages which depend on the well bucket or outside pump. A machine designed for digging trenches across open country has been applied to opening the stub-

159

born roads for the laying of the pipes, and though it has been heroically battling with iron-hard surfaces against which it was never meant to fight, it is making slow progress and holding up traffic magnificently. Whether it has seen active service I do not know, but as peace goes, it deserves mention in dispatches for the bravery with which it returns to the charge after breaking down in contest with fearful odds. Once, indeed, it caught fire and was thought out of action for good, but at the moment of writing it has returned to fight on. One day, therefore, I shall scrap my well and pump and trust in that centralization which is both the blessing and curse of our civilized world, so convenient in ordinary times, and so devastating when anything goes wrong.

Mineral waters provide a technical subject on which the writer is peculiarly qualified to pontificate as he knows nothing whatever about them. Turning to Simon's invaluable *Encyclopædia*, he finds that they are 'spring waters which are impregnated with mineral salts to which they owe their medicinal value, if any, and their individual flavour.' Some years ago I went to the Pyrenees and passed through the ordeal of a cure for catarrh, which involved the swallowing and sniffing up of a quantity of naturally hot and naturally nasty waters, bubbling up in pump rooms and a swimming bath, as well as trickling out of rocks. My conviction that this proceeding was as useless as it was unpleasant did not prevent me going conscientiously through the routine; of course, it did no good to my catarrh, which stopped instantly when I gave up smoking. At any rate Cauterets was a pleasant place to swagger about in from one radio-active spring to another with a small tumbler in a basket case slung across one's shoulder, and when I had done with obeisance to the mumbo-jumbo of Aesculapius, I had a very delightful scramble over to the Spanish side of the mountains. I wonder if the Pyrenees have once again had their share of snow. At that time, there had been a decade in which the snow-line had been ascending the slopes and precipices, and the glaciers had been shrinking in the most tragic fashion. The mention of Pyrenean waters has called to my mind a memory of Vichy. I was still on the *Morning Post* when I travelled to that watering-place to inaugurate a new Pullman service intended to encourage the wealthy to grow healthy by patronizing its healing waters. Lord Dalziel was in charge, and the train fairly flowed with milk and honey to stimulate the journalistic pen, but Vichy water only made its appearance on our arrival; for my bedroom in the hotel was equipped with the only free bottle of Vichy Celestins I have ever seen.

A visit to Lourdes, where the waters of the miraculous spring are held more precious than wine, was brought to my memory, when I came across, in a book on Gnosticism, *Fragments of a Faith Forgotten*, the account of a curious, not to say topsy-turvy, rite. Two wine-jars are set out on the altar which is decorated with symbolic vine and olive branches, and after due ceremonial the mysterious priest Melchisidec is summoned to transform the wine in the wine-jars into water for the baptism of the initiates. Orthodox Christians have incurred considerable expense in transporting from the Jordan water for the baptism of their children, and in a famous London cellar some bottles of this fluid imported for the christening of royal babies are binned away—I think they are kept lying on their side —cheek by jowl with great wines of famous vintages. Yet a miracle to convert the fermented juice of the grape into the liquid to which it must after the vinegar state ultimately return, would seem spendthrift waste of the miraculous, and an inexcusable extravagance, which may well account for the verdict of heresy returned against *The Book of the Gnoses of the Invisible God*, which describes the ceremony. The alchemists, it is true, hoped to extract the quintessence and perfection of life by their distillation of wine, but they found alcohol, not water, and we may be pretty sure that the Gnostics would not have thought of their miracle unless they had wished to challenge the orthodox miracle of the marriage at Cana. Most of them were extreme ascetics and had no sympathy with Paul's advice to Timothy: 'Drink no longer water, but use a little wine for thy stomach's sake and thine often infirmities.'

I spoke above of washing teeth in Paris with Eau St. Galmier, and indeed there were luxurious folk who took baths in it when the town water smelt very bad. It was soda water, Chesterton's 'torment for our crimes,' that inspired T. S. Eliot with the grisly picture of 'The Fire Sermon' in *The Waste Land*.

> O the moon shone bright on Mrs. Porter
> And on her daughter
> They wash their feet in soda-water.

Since musings on water have carried me to the poets, Chesterton is bound to occupy the forefront of my thought:

> Feast on wine or fast on water
> And your honour shall stand sure,
> God Almighty's son and daughter,
> He the valiant, she the pure!

It was, I think, rather lip-service than true homage that G. K. C. paid to the Almighty's daughter; at least Noah treated her very cavalierly when he kept exclaiming that he didn't care where the water went if it didn't get into the wine, and the Curse of Water being on us yet because of the wrath of God scarcely squares with aqueous enthusiasm.

In childhood I was immensely impressed by the Scandinavian god—was it Thor, or Odin?—who nearly drank up the sea. He was prepared to swallow at one draught the contents of the largest conceivable drinking horn, and some crafty challenger arranged that the horn supplied for the competition should draw for its contents on the ocean. I have probably got the story wrong after so many years, but it ran after that fashion, and I felt that I had struck the same legend when my eyes fell on two admirable stanzas from Aytoun's *Massacre of the Macpherson*.

162

Fhairson had a son,
    Who married Noah's daughter,
And nearly spoiled ta Flood,
    By trinking up ta water:
Which he would have done,
    I at least pelieve it,
Had the mixture peen
    Only half Glenlivet.

Austerity had not been thought of in those happy days, when it was possible to think, yes, even to think, of half the volume of the Flood being Scotch Whisky, so much there was of it at three or four shillings a bottle. I am no whisky fanatic, but I have known times when a whisky and soda pleased as nothing else could, and to my mind the best mineral water for the mixing was Mattoni, Giesshübler, a non-alcoholic blending mixture which I have never known equalled and which seems to have utterly disappeared. It distresses me in Simon's *Encyclopaedia* that the spelling of *whisky* for Scotland and *whiskey* for Ireland receives no notice, and there is no heading for Fhairson's *Glenlivet*. So I turn to that classic work *Whisky* by Aeneas MacDonald and find that the Glen Elgin-Glenlivet distillery claims to possess the finest distilling water in Scotland, drawn from a mountain spring. It relies upon 'the finest and purest water on earth, which tumbles down the mountainside for 1,200 feet, and glides through the district in the sparkling stream of Livet.' Here at least I have an opportunity of glorifying water without providing the *black teetotaller* with ammunition. If we are able today just to keep our heads above water by the exportation of Scotch Whisky to the land of dollars, it is because water, peat and barley condition the taste of the distilled spirit. Livet water is ideal, because it is devoid of all mineral contamination— that is what they call in Scotland the much-advertised salts of famous spas—and gives no extraneous flavour to the malt it makes. MacDonald tells a story of a distillery and

163

a famous burn flowing from a mountainside renowned for whisky, which finds a suitable place in a chapter devoted to H_2O. For the sake of that burn a distillery was built at great expense in a West Highland seaport. 'The water was all that could be wished for. It was clear and sparkling to the eye, pleasant to the palate, triumphant in the laboratory. But alas! It had one fault. Good whisky could not be made from it. Chemists, maltsters and stillmen could try as they might; it was of no avail. The money, it seemed, had been as good as thrown away.'

About a mile away there was a mean little stream running off the same hillside with none of the other burn's attractions, and when the latter defied all efforts to convert it to alcoholic association, a despairing experiment was tried with the former. The miracle happened in the shape of a whisky of the highest quality, and the water of that unassuming, unattractive stream is now the parent of a valuable spirit.

So much for water as a beverage or as part of a beverage; it is more useful for our endeavours to climb the peak of cleanliness, which we know stands next to the mountain of godliness. The wise reproach of the Italian priest to the novice who came to Rome with a tin bath in his luggage has not been obliterated even by the merciless sponge of war: 'My son, when you have attained to godliness, then it will be time to think of cleanliness.' The water from my well claims a place very near the throne of pre-eminence in the matter of hardness. It is strange how one is prone to boast of excess in one's possessions even when it is a lamentable fault which distinguishes them. At any rate, my water is said by the experts, who should know, to have forty-eight degrees of hardness out of a possible record fifty, and the money I have spent in putting in softeners has been a dead loss. Only through large rainwater tanks have our lives been saved, though there is no contrivance by which soft water can be conveyed to our baths. Yet even so I can understand the affection with which Rupert Brooke spoke of 'the benison of hot water.'

> The cool kindliness of sheets, that soon
> Smooth away trouble; and the rough male kiss of
>   blankets.

O that comfortable bed that follows the hot bath! Only Catullus has told more exquisitely of the delight of returning home after a long journey. 'What rapture equals that release from care? When the mind drops its load and we come home from the travail of our travels, and sink into the bed of our heart's desire.'

How preferable to me is hot water in a bath to iced water in a pitcher, that cold comfort which our American cousins enjoy after the cocktail! It is, as Simon says somewhere, the death of all good cookery to have nothing to drink with a meal and that habit seems to grow more and more widely spread. Doctors attribute the indigestion of pre-prandial drinks to liquid accompaniment of food, and when there is no wine, they can scarcely be gainsaid. Iced water will ever be remembered by me for the tip given to the bellboy for the pitcher, which was the standing order on arrival in an hotel. It was in those days, thirty years ago, the only visible product for which a dime was sufficient remuneration; I suppose nowadays a dollar is insufficient.

In this country no one would think of paying anyone sixpence for bringing a jug of iced water to a bedroom, and our disrespect for that fluid finds expression in the technical terms of the wine trade. After all, spirits have to be broken down and only water is appropriate for their tempering, but the cellar-man carries out his duty as though it were a guilty secret and disguises the operation by the camouflage of distilled water under the name of *liquor*.

'Stolen waters are sweet, and bread eaten in secret is pleasant,' the author of the Proverbs of Solomon undoubtedly knew human nature to its depths and had a

165

quite unregal sympathy with people who did things on the sly and enjoyed them all the more for their low cunning. 'Stolen waters' I fear, do not refer to strong or Barbados waters, such as delighted our ancestors' and some of our ancestresses' hearts, but rather to the tapping of a spring in a country where no water is. In the East, water indeed comes into its own for its scarcity, and those whom the Prophet forbids to drink wine would find no reason for surprise in those weather conditions which sometimes in France, notably in Champagne in 1893, made water dearer than wine. In Fez, the City of the Waters, all life depends on the supply of water drawn from the river which flows down through the steep town, providing it with refreshment and carrying off all its impurities, and few crafts had more importance than the guild of the water overseers, who carried in their heads the detailed map of all the water conduits, private and public, which had maintained the city's needs for a thousand years. Equally well considered were those Arabs in the Sahara, who could divine in the oases the spots where water would soonest be struck and a pit sunk perhaps three hundred feet would eventually find the great underground rivers which flow beneath the desert.

Water-divining is a curious gift which the scientist has still to explain. Ravenhill of *Punch* had a friend now dead who was a skilled dowser, and took me to see him at work in Surrey. We dodged water, silver, and gold objects about in a ground-floor room of his house and from the storey above he followed their movement with perfect accuracy and the divining rod told him their exact position. He gave me a hawthorn twig to try my hand at the game and to my surprise it moved in my hands with no volition of mine so far as I could feel. On three occasions it indicated spots of ground where we found water quite near the surface and I am convinced that there was not so much water under his garden that it was a pure chance that the rod was right on the only three occasions I put it to the test.

IV

Glimpses in Austerity of By-Gone Luxury

URING these days when one has nothing better to wash down a meal than the memory of a wine drunk in happier times, it is consoling to note references to good cheer in the past, when even in Lent austerity was tempered ·for men of religion by good cooking and plenty of wine, as often as one stumbles upon them in casual reading, and treat them as good augury for the future after the fashion of the *Sortes Virgilianae*. Possibly an outcry against luxury is rather a backhanded kind of encouragement, but the denunciation of a sin does not always deprive it of its temptation. Certainly I did not expect to find anything that would provide a gastronomical text, when I took up *Sesame and Lilies*, the lectures of that not excessively virile aesthete and wine-merchant, John Ruskin, with the immediate intention of refreshing my memory of his comments on Milton's *Lycidas*. For the moment I had forgotten that he was a wine-merchant and the son of a wine-merchant, who, happy man! spent two months travelling each year in his carriage to collect orders for his firm. They drove their leisurely way of forty or fifty miles a day, a stage or two before breakfast 'with the dew on the grass and first scent from the hawthorns,' reaching their goal in time for four o'clock dinner, after

167

many deviations to great houses with cellars that might want stocking. How right Ruskin was, when he wrote in *Modern Painters*: 'There was always more in the world than men could see, walked they never so slowly; they will see it no better for going fast.' I long ago knew what it was to see Italy from a one-horse shay, tasting the vintages of the wine country in their homes, and then discovered that the trains which Ruskin loathed and despised moved much too fast for acquaintance with the country through which they passed. What Ruskin would have done about the motor-cars, with their saving of so many hours, which their passengers have to idle away because they have no idea what to do with them, defies imagination. Probably he would have gone out with a pick-axe to make good wholesome holes, in the main roads, of a depth to break a spring, or potted dangerous drivers from behind a hedge with a shot gun. It might have tickled his fancy to know that when speed on the roads was slaying its thousands our representatives should be worrying more about the blood sports that kill a certain number of animals than the Great Blood Sport, as Kipling called it, of running down pedestrians; not indeed that Ruskin would have sympathized with the fox-hunters, for he was anything but a sportsman and I have a vague memory that he poured ridicule on the Boat Race. He would have applauded Wilde's description of the man in pink as 'the unspeakable in pursuit of the uneatable.' Undoubtedly, however, if he were alive today, he would agree with me that the aeroplane has introduced the perfect *reductio ad absurdum* of Travel, which Bacon tells us should be 'in the younger Sort, a Part of Education; in the Elder, a Part of Experience.' Let an aircraft be flown round the world back to its starting-point without stopping, and the ideal of the speed maniac is in sight. It is possible to fly round the world in a closed box, seeing and learning nothing of its variety, at a vertiginous speed. It only remains to keep on doing so indefinitely. What more could the traveller demand, though I fear that his revolution round the earth after the fashion of the moon, will scarcely allow him to take Bacon's advice and 'prick in some Flowers, of that he hath Learned abroad, into the Customes of his own Country.'

Once again digression has led me astray, and I have still to come to the kernel of the nut which *Sesame and Lilies* offers to the crackers. To a disquisition on English poverty in the 'sixties, which fills him with fierce and righteous indignation, Ruskin appends a quotation from the *Morning Post* of March 10, 1865, which seems to have very little to do with the matter, as it deals with Paris, but is in itself of interest to the writer. Between forty and fifty years later I was the Paris Correspondent of this newspaper, and the cutting which Ruskin consigned to what he called his store-drawer as a horrible example of luxury came from the pen of one of my predecessors in this office. It was actually Oliver Borthwick, who afterwards became Lord Glenesk and proprietor of the *Morning Post*. He gave his approval to my appointment, when I went out to succeed *Saki* Munro, and it was always a thorn in my side that in those spacious days of the Second Empire he had managed to frequent the highest and most luxurious circles of luxurious Paris on a salary of £200 a year. On this occasion he discreetly discloses to his fashionable readers the goings-on in 'the *salons* of Mme C——,' a lady, who I fear was no better than she should be and 'who did the honours with clever imitative grace and elegance.' Her rooms were crowded with princes, dukes, marquises, and counts, 'in fact with the same *male* company as one meets at the parties of the Princess Metternich and Madame Drouyn de Lhuys. Some English peers and members of Parliament were present, and appeared to enjoy the animated and dazzlingly improper scene.'

'That your readers,' continues the Correspondent, who had obviously shared the enjoyment of the peers and

169

M.P.s, 'may form some idea of the dainty fare of the Parisian *demi-monde*, I copy the menu of the supper, which was served to all the guests (about 200) seated at four o'clock. Choice Yquem, Johannisberg, Laffitte (O my great and to-be-ennobled Predecessor, did you so mis-spell Château Lafite; perish the thought, it must have been the printer!), Tokay, and Champagne of the finest vintages were served most lavishly throughout the morning. After supper dancing was resumed with increased animation, and the ball terminated with a *chaîne diabolique* and a *cancan d'enfer* at seven in the morning. Here is the menu: "Consommé de volaille à la Bagration; sixteen hors d'œuvres variés. Bouchées à la Talleyrand. Saumons froids, sauce Ravigote. Filets de bœuf en Bellevue, timbales milanaises, chaudfroid de gibier. Dindes truffées. Pâtés de foie gras, buissons d'écrevisses, salades vénitiennes, gelées blanches aux fruits, gâteaux mancini, parisiens et parisiennes. Fromages. Glaces. Ananas. Dessert".'

It is sad to think how grieved Ruskin would be at the thought that this orgiacal gobbet, embalmed as a denunciatory warning against 'the raptures and roses of vice,' should be exhumed to bring water to the mouths of the ascetics of compulsory austerity, and to remind the writer that he was born too late into a world too old, or at any rate missed a lot in not becoming a journalist in Paris before the downfall of the Second Empire, though it must be said that the Third Republic was not entirely devoid of the attractions of the world, the flesh and the devil.

Reaction from this long colloquy with Ruskin carried me to a more robust and heretical philosopher, the American, Ralph Waldo Emerson, who, to judge from his poem entitled *Bacchus*, entertained some ideas about wine quite out of the common. The reader will remember that in his enthusiasm for the Pantheism of the East he sang:

> I am the doubter and the doubt,
> And I the hymn the Brahmin sings,

inspiring Andrew Lang with his pleasant parody:

> I am the batsman and the bat,
> I am the bowler and the ball,
> The umpire, the pavilion cat,
> The roller, pitch, and stumps, and all.

In the light of the universal mystical identity, it becomes manifest that Emerson's *Bacchus* celebrates not the stuff the vintner sells, but some spiritual beverage which perhaps may be poured in the inn at the end of the world. For he calls for wine 'which never grew in the belly of the grape,' or else grew on a vine, which presumably had no fear of the phylloxera since it can scarcely have been grafted on an American stock; for its tap-roots reached 'through under the Andes to the Cape' and suffered 'no savour of the earth to 'scape.' It is distinctly unusual for a wine-drinker to have such a craving for the *terroir* tang, and I cannot think that delicacy will be enhanced if the grapes come 'from a nocturnal root which feels the acrid juice of Styx and Erebus.'

Our poet complains of buying ashes for bread and diluted wine; and what he wants is

> Wine of wine,
> Blood of the world,
> Form of forms, and mould of statures,
> That I intoxicated,
> And by the draught assimilated,
> May float at pleasure through all natures;
> The bird-language rightly spell,
> And that which roses say so well.

After this it is not surprising to be told that this wine 'is already man,' and also Music, and that he thanks the joyful juice for all he knows. So he ends with an appeal to the Wine-God,

> Pour, Bacchus! the remembering wine;
> Retrieve the loss of me and mine!
> Vine for vine be antidote,
> And the grape requite the lote!

171

Somehow I wish Emerson could have found a rhyme without giving to the Lethean Lotos which bestows forgetfulness the pet-name of *lote*. He is not so frank as that dear little girl Marjorie Fleming who died at the age of eight and wrote the following poem to a dog.

> O lovely, O most charming pug
> Thy graceful air and heavenly mug . . .
> His noses cast is of the roman
> He is a very pretty weoman
> I could not get a rhyme for roman
> And was obliged to call it weoman.

I almost think that this young lady whose sincerity made her confess in her Journal, 'Today I pronounced a word which should never come out of a lady's lips it was that I called John a Impudent Bitch,' might have helped Emerson straighten out his ideas about wine in her downright way, though as that wise traveller and War Correspondent Percival Phillips would have said, 'It is all very difficult.'

My next note carries us back to Dryden, and I must admit that I am in doubt whether the views he intended to express in his early poem *Astraea Redux* about wine are really much more sound than those of Emerson, though in later years when he had become 'Glorious John' he probably had a good deal more practice as wine-bibber, consuming his daily bottle at Will's Coffee-house. In the passage which attracted my attention, he apologizes to Charles II so happily restored for the disloyalty shown by him and his friends in the days of the Commonwealth. Dryden had been Secretary to Sir Gilbert Pickering his uncle, who was Cromwell's right-hand man.

> . . . as those lees that trouble it refine
> The agitated soul of generous wine,
> So tears of joy, for your returning spilt,
> Work out and expiate our former guilt.

Tears of joy may work out Dryden's guilt, but I cannot

172

quite work out the parallel with the wine lees. Presumably they refine the wine, when it is racked off them, and I suppose that the agitation must refer to the beating up of the wine with the finings. Dryden was nearly thirty at the time, so that he was not a novice in the art of wine-drinking, but he was a new hand at poetry and so probably did not quite work out his simile.

A less known and rather older poet, Thomas Jordan, who flourished in Dryden's lifetime, celebrated the Restoration rejoicings in a jolly, carefree song that deserves quotation.

> Let us drink and be merry, dance, joke, and rejoice,
> With claret and sherry, theorbo and voice!
> The changeable world to our joy is unjust,
>   All treasure's uncertain,
>   Then down with your dust!
> In frolics dispose your pounds, shillings and pence,
> For we shall be nothing a hundred years hence.
>
> We'll sport and be free with Moll, Betty and Dolly,
> Have oysters and lobsters to cure melancholy:
> Fish-dinners will make a man spring like a flea,
>   Dame Venus, love's lady,
>   Was born of the sea:
> With her and with Bacchus we'll tickle the sense,
> For we shall be past it a hundred years hence.

It is pretty certain that after austerity and controls there will be a reaction to luxury and licence as there was at the swing over from Puritanism to the Restoration; for human nature does not change. In Russia they seem to temper the tyranny of labour for the dictatorial proletariat, not only with the auxiliary relief of millions of slaves outside the law, but also with the *panem et circenses* of drama and music, and plenty of vodka. Here a cry is raised if grandmotherly legislation allows the money-maker to sit up till 2 a.m. and have a drink to keep him awake. Claret and Sherry may come our way again, if not the theorbo, described in the dictionary as a two-necked instrument of the lute class, and we may even try to dispel melancholy with oysters and lobsters, but generally speaking this country is suffering from a glut of fish and whatever its amatory value, there is more likely to be a cry for meat and sweets than for the fruit of the sea.

Abraham Cowley also survived the end of Puritanism and finds the world full of reasons to justify the Quaker's Chorus that the more we drink together the merrier we shall be. In his *Anacreontics* he points out that the thirsty earth drinks up the rain, the plants also, the sea drinks up the rivers, the sun the sea, the moon and stars the sun, though how they do it he does not explain. He winds up:

> Nothing in Nature's sober found,
> But an eternal health goes round.
> Fill up the bowl, then, fill it high,
> Fill all the glasses there—for why
> Should every creature drink but I?
> Why, man of morals, tell me why?

Less sophisticated and of an earlier date comes an anonymous song in praise of Tobacco and Ale. The Moors describe smoking as drinking the forbidden, and this early rhymester encourages his readers to 'drink Tobacco' with much sententious moralizing to excuse the indulgence. The withered Indian weed reminds us that all flesh is hay: 'Thus think, then drink Tobacco.' The smoke shows the vanity of worldly stuff, gone with a puff: 'Thus think, then drink Tobacco.' A foul pipe denotes the soul foul with sin and the fire it needs to cleanse it: 'Thus think, then drink Tobacco.'

> The ashes, that are left behind,
> May serve to put thee still in mind
> That unto dust return thou must:
> Thus think, then drink Tobacco.

Our poet had to find excuses for the outlandish and new-fangled vice of smoking. Maybe he lived late enough to read James I's *Counterblast to Tobacco* and so see his

174

pseudo-pious conceits disposed of by the description of the habit as 'a branch of the sin of drunkenness, which is the root of all sins.' It was a bold smoker who sought to point a moral by reading lessons of life in 'a custom loathsome to the eye, hateful to the nose, harmful to the brain, dangerous to the lungs, and in the black, stinking fume thereof, nearest resembling the horrible Stygian smoke of the pit that is bottomless.' Again it was difficult to appear virtuous when recommending an addiction, which made the King exclaim: 'Herein is not only a great vanity, but a great contempt of God's good gifts, that the sweetness of man's breath, being a good gift of God, should be wilfully corrupted by this stinking smoke.' There is something to be said for the French king's description of James as 'the wisest fool in Christendom.'

Our apologist for Tobacco drops all his moralizing, when he leaves 'the Indian weed' and turns to the glorification of Ale. Ale, he feels, is so obviously good in itself, indeed beyond all praise, that it would be mere impertinence to make excuses for it and its benedictions. 'Give me Ale,' he cries, 'when as the chill Charokko blows,' and when 'the birds sit cursing of the frosts and snows.' Our panegyrist of Ale must have travelled far afield to have discovered the Scirocco, though his spelling of the word is as eccentric as his conception of its nature; for the Scirocco is not a chill wind, but a dry parching wind from the Sahara. Still he can hardly have learned the name without travelling into wine countries, and his loyalty to the Ale of his country is the more touching. Certainly there is much to be said for 'Ale in a Saxon rumkin, such as will make grimalkin prate.' I am afraid our friend from the past would have a long way to look in the present before he found any form of beer that would made a cat talkative. Nor can I say of the pint that I may have at the local that it tells mortal wights what's done and past, and what's to come. Our breweries seem to have mislaid the gift of prophecy and modern beer

175

is not strong enough to make one think that one is a prophet.

Milton tells of 'the spicy nutbrown Ale,' and that no doubt was the Ale, which we are told by our anonymous poet, 'the plowman's heart upkeeps and equals it with tyrants' thrones,' to say nothing of wiping the eye that overweeps, and lulling 'in sure and dainty sleeps th' oe'r-wearied bones.'

We learn from Shakespeare that a quart of ale is a dish for a king, and Farquhar in *The Beaux Stratagem* whets one's thirst for Audit Ale with promise of an *Anno Domini,* which was presumably brewed the year of its brewer's birth, as in Victorian times a pipe of Port was laid down when the heir was born for drinking when he came of age. It was a true Ale-lover who said in the same play: 'I have fed purely upon Ale; I have eat my Ale, drank my Ale, and I always sleep upon Ale.' If my memory is correct, it was Mr. Boniface who thus summed up his life. Even so he scarcely outdoes in his enthusiasm the poet whose verses on wine and tobacco have inspired the last lines of this chapter:

> Grandchild of Ceres, Bacchus' daughter,
>   Wine's emulous neighbour, though but stale,
> Ennobling all the nymphs of water,
>   And filling each man's heart with laughter—
>   Ha! give me ale!

176

V

The Art of Good Living and a Dictionary of Quotations

IN the last chapter, perhaps my optimism erred, when I spoke of the consolation to be derived from treating the records of past good cheer as omens of good living yet to come. Grievous is the memory of plenty in time of scarcity, or so the wise men say. Dante when he breaks his reader's heart with the love of Paolo and Francesca, seems to attribute the sentiment that there is no greater pain than the remembrance of happiness in time of misery to his beloved master Virgil, though Boëthius was really responsible for it, declaring in his ponderous Latin, *in omni adversitate fortunae infelicissimum genus infortunii est fuisse felicem*. Boëthius languishing to death in his dungeon was no doubt an expert on the matter; yet perhaps a certain wistful pleasure may be found in the recollection of happier days all the more welcome if it carries with it a hope that they may come again. The gift of *The Oxford Dictionary of Quotations* came as an exhortation to literary nostalgic musings of the past, and as a wine-lover I turned to its pages hoping for a wealth of extracts dealing with the fermented juice of the grape in all its forms.

Chance opened the volume at the page of the Index on which Burgundy should have been inscribed, but the name was not there and further search disclosed no mention of Hock or Rhenish, surely literary wines, if ever any were. Not a word about Bordeaux, but two references for Claret: the first, Dr. Johnson's too often repeated remark, 'Claret is the liquor for boys; Port for men; but he who aspires to be a hero must drink Brandy.' There seems little more point in the dictum that strong men should drink strong drinks than in the line 'Who rules o'er freemen should himself be free,' which Johnson caricatured with 'Who drives fat oxen should himself be fat.'

The second reference to Claret is equally impolite to the queen of wines. We are told of that great classical scholar Richard Bentley—'He is believed to have liked Port, but to have said of Claret that *it would be Port if it could.*' Bentley died in 1742, so that he belonged to the period when Etonians drank *blackstrap* and Dr. Warner, Selwyn's toady, swilled Port with his food and drank fine Claret or Burgundy after eating. No wonder Claret seemed to them *wishwashy* stuff. Yet it was not so very much later that Beau Brummell could affect a highly supercilious attitude towards the Englishman's wine, though it was only to snub an officious busybody who wanted to know whether the King of the Dandies approved of Port. 'Port?' he replied in a puzzled tone. 'Port? What! the hot intoxicating liquor so much drunk by the lower orders?' How genuine was this assumed contempt was revealed by the contents of his cellar put up for sale at Christie's, when he fled from his creditors in 1815. The main lot consisted of ten dozen of Capital Old Port, which sold at 80s. the dozen.

Naturally, after this, my next inquiry into the Index was directed to Port and I rejoiced to find more than a dozen entries. I felt confident that I should find among them my favourite quotation from *The Egoist*, in which Meredith's Dr. Middleton talks of Senatorial Port, ancient Hermitage and senior Hocks, but alas! I found it not. It had not struck me that *port* is a most equivocal word. We can talk of *any*

178

port in a storm and Cleopatra of her *sprightly port* without any suggestion of the only Port worthy of a capital initial, the fortified wine of the Upper Douro shipped over the Bar of Oporto. This definition eliminates all but three of the Index references, and too of these concern the relations of Port and Claret and have already been dealt with. Only one extract adds anything to our knowledge, but that unquestionably deserves quotation. It comes from the pen of the Reverend R. H. Barham, the author of the *Ingoldsby Legends*.

> Though Port should have age,
>   Yet I don't think it sage
> To entomb it, as some of your *connoisseurs* do,
> Till it's losing its flavour, and body, and hue;
> I question if keeping does it much good
> After ten years in bottle and three in the wood.

Here Ingoldsby throws down the gauntlet to a host of wine-lovers, and meets with the approval of Saintsbury in his *Notes to a Cellar-Book*. The Professor singularly enough supposes the rule applies more generally to Claret than Port, though I think the modern school usually regards the finest Clarets as at least as long-lived as Port. Certainly a bottle of 1912 Fonseca which came my way the other day showed no sign at all of losing either its flavour, body or colour.

I was rewarded for turning up Champagne by five quotations all dealing with the wine and not the province. First of all I was confronted with that familiar passage from *Handley Cross* in which the sparkling wine—supposedly of luxury—finds itself in very strange company and employed for a very strange purpose. 'Bishops' boots Mr. Radcliffe also condemned, and spoke highly in favour of tops cleaned with Champagne and abricot jam.' The second was also from Surtees: 'Champagne certainly gives one werry gentlemanly ideas, but for a continuance, I don't know but I should prefer mild hale.' So *Mr. Jorrocks in Paris*.

The last person I expected to meet in my search for

179

literary allusions to wine was that incorrigible apostle of austerity George Bernard Shaw, but even he has his contribution to make to an Anthology of Dionysus. There is something to tickle the fancy in the phrase, 'I'm only a beer teetotaler, not a Champagne teetotaller,' which is to be found in the Third Act of *Candida*. From Bernard Shaw we pass to *The Lover* of the sprightly and adventurous Lady Mary Wortley Montagu, who calls up in a single line a cosy picture of a *tête-à-tête*.

And we meet, with Champagne and a chicken, at last.

Finally Belloc, that lover of Burgundy, is at his best in *On a Great Election*.

> The accursed power which stands on Privilege
> (And goes with Women, and Champagne, and Bridge)
> Broke—and Democracy resumed her reign:
> (Which goes with Bridge, and Women, and Champagne).

Madeira finds no more place in these Oxford extracts from English literature than Poins' query to Falstaff, 'Jack! how agrees the devil and thee about thy soul, that thou soldest him on Good Friday last for a cup of Madeira and a cold capon's leg?' Canary wine no longer appears in Wine Lists, but Ben Jonson made it sound very seductive, when he was inviting a friend to supper.

> But that which most doth take my Muse and me,
> Is a pure cup of rich Canary wine,
> Which is the Mermaid's now, but shall be mine:
> Of which, had Horace or Anacreon tasted,
> Their lives, as do their lines, till now had lasted.

The rich immortal perfume of the Mermaid Canary embalms Keats' imagination.

> Souls of poets dead and gone,
> What Elysium have ye known,
> Happy field or mossy cavern,
> Choicer than the Mermaid Tavern?
> Have ye tippled drink more fine
> Than mine host's Canary wine?

180

I must confess for myself that, if the day ever comes for the fulfilment of missing experience, I should put in a pressing plea to taste that wine of poetry and romance, and how happy would one be if it was permitted for just one night to join the sacred company in Elysium,

> Pledging with contented smack
> The Mermaid in the Zodiac.

· Having exhausted the references to particular wines, as many as I could think of at random, I turned my attention to spirits, Brandy, of course, having pride of place as a derivative of wine should. Inevitably I was faced again by Dr. Johnson and his brandy-drinking hero: then I could join in the smuggler's chorus with Rudyard Kipling, 'Brandy for the Parson, 'Baccy for the Clerk,' remembering those happier days when the strictest control could not put an end to the running of contraband. It seems to me improbable that Elia was very serious, when he wrote:

> If ever I marry a wife,
>   I'll marry the landlord's daughter,
> For then I may sit in the bar,
>   And drink cold Brandy and water.

I have little enthusiasm for Brandy and water, whether hot or cold, but it seems to have been an inspiriting drink, when it was fashionable. We have it on the authority of the Georgian dramatist, George Colman, that 'Mynheer Vandunck, though he never was drunk, sipped Brandy and water gaily.' Finally Robert Burns assures us somewhat cynically that 'There's some are fou o' love divine, There's some are fou o' Brandy.'

This same Scottish poet provides, as is not perhaps unnatural, our only authority on whisky, and I am quite horrified to observe that the Index has fallen into the hairraising error of spelling it whiskey, as if Burns wrote in Erse. The pathetic lament of *The Author's Earnest Cry and Prayer*, when he asked for whisky's name in Greek and

181

swore that 'Freedom and whisky gang thegither,' would come home nowadays to more than Scotsmen. Then he and his countrymen were breathing fire and slaughter at Pitt's enforcement of the Excise Laws, which threatened to put the illicit still out of business. Burns cried to high heaven 'of mine an' Scotland's drouth,' but nowadays there is such a drought of Scotch everywhere on this side of the Atlantic as he could never have conceived.

Gin can scarcely be described as an inspiring subject for poet and prose writer; depression and mother's ruin are its family names, though it conceals its sadness behind a manifold of confused tastes in the cocktail as if the skeleton at the feast had been consigned to an adjacent cupboard. In *Guy Mannering*, the smuggler may sing, 'Gin by pailfuls, wine in rivers, Dash the window-glass to shivers,' but the reckless gaiety lacks conviction. It was of no praiseworthy merrymaking that A. P. Herbert wrote when he prayed the world:

> Don't tell my twin that I breakfast on gin,
> He'd never survive the blow.

Here surely the Anthology might have added the historic disagreement between Clerihew and Dr. Clifford, the one disapproving of gin, the other of sin. Kipling, however, is included, confining gin and beer to home service and setting in its place the water brought by Gunga Din, when it came to overseas slaughter.

Rum as the pet name of the ancient Rumbullion sounded more promising as a stimulant to the English writer, for it has been called the Englishman's spirit, since it was he who realized the possibilities of the fermented sugar cane. The Anthology could not overlook Stevenson with his 'Yo-ho-ho, and a bottle of rum,' and my hopes brightened when I read the entry 'Rum on the port.' This sounded like a mixture of drinks belonging to the age of heroic barbarians with constitutions which could make light of the iron stomachs and heads that we weaklings are accustomed to attribute to Russians. What kind of rum I wondered and my thoughts wandered to the terrific Rumbullion, reeking of tar, oakum and fiery spirit, which in the days of Prohibition was smuggled into Newfoundland from St. Pierre Miquelon to save its inhabitants from a beverage of blacking, the only other liquid obtainable containing a percentage of alcohol. My disappointment was great when I discovered that I had been once again deceived by verbal equivocation. The reference was again to Stevenson, but there was no question of a bottle of Rumbullion, but merely of a northern island: 'Mull was astern, Rum on the port, Eigg on the starboard bow.'

The other two references to rum most oddly connect it with religion. First we have Byron in *Don Juan* taking a favourable, if flippant, view of the soothing virtues of the sugar cane spirit! 'There's nought, no doubt, so much the spirit calms As rum and true religion.' On the other hand, Samuel Dickenson Burchard, of whom I know nothing except that he seems to have been an American who lived from 1812 to 1891 and made a speech in New York City on October 29, 1884, declaring, 'We are Republicans and don't propose to leave our party and identify ourselves with the party whose antecedents are rum, Romanism and rebellion.'

A casual dip into the Index was rewarded by a remark ascribed to J. L. Motley, the historian, in Oliver Wendell Holmes' *Autocrat of the Breakfast Table*: 'Give us the luxuries of life, and we will dispense with the necessities.' Such a sentiment rings with a delightfully shocking peal in ears trained to the dull puritanical strains of austerity. The quarrel as to where the line should be drawn between luxuries and necessities will never be made up. Keats brooded over Fanny Brawne's loveliness and the hour of his death as 'two luxuries' which he yearned to possess 'both in the same minute,' and perhaps he gave a short list of his necessities when he wrote that same year to Fanny: 'Give me books, fruit, french wine and fine weather, and a little music out of doors, played by somebody I do not know.' At least all these things may be taken by a poet as necessary to that refined and appreciative existence at which presumably all civilizations aim. John Bright said in 1886 that the knowledge of the ancient languages is mainly a luxury and to all appearances this view has prevailed, though I for one will fight against it to the last ditch. There was a moment when in a tiny city state the mind of man reached a zenith of critical understanding and sensitive appreciation, an ability to think and to create beauty, that it has never since approached, and recorded that miracle in a language that fringes perfection as no other tongue has ever done. Can it be said that knowledge of that Golden Age and that golden speech is *mainly a luxury*? Only in the Dark Ages.

I would hazard the guess that the wiseacres who sniff contemptuously at 'fancy' cheeses as though Roquefort was made to be smelled and not eaten, also turn up their noses at classical languages and would be almost insulted by one of those great quotations, which so often flashed through the Parliamentary debates of the past with the glory of a ray of sunlight. *Fancy* cheese, the epithet betrays the lie in the soul that belongs to the prisoner who has never seen light outside the dungeons of the town. Such people believe that Nature arranges for water to flow from taps, light to be produced by the snapping of a switch, and food to grow in tins. Plain or simple cheese they are convinced should be churned out by the mass production of Mother Nature from any form of grease, whether derived from a cow, goat, or motor sump, unvarying in appearance and tastelessness and wrapped in silver paper by natural forces. Divine equality must not be broken and blasphemed by a multiplicity of cheeses, any more than by the birth of men with different coloured hair and various dispositions. The *Internationale*, if it is rightly understood, proclaims the right of all the world to *mouse-trap* and nothing better; the cheese that baits the mouse-trap is the cheese that feeds the world. For some reason unexplained, it is more virtuous and patriotic to swallow down a Transatlantic imitation of Cheddar than pleasurably to indulge in the sophistication of Camembert, Roquefort or Stilton. The inhabitants of Gorgonzola, that village on the outskirts of Milan, would be astonished to learn that the curse of luxury and debauch lay heavy on their labours when they were making their famous green cheese and that Punch's renowned war-cry, 'Hi! James—let loose the Gorgonzola!' has become in this country as subversive a slogan of high treason as 'Up the Reds!' or any summons to battle devised by the imagination of rebel Irishmen. Maybe they might hope to escape our Ministerial damnation if they confined their occupation to the making of *stracchino di Milano*, a white cheese of the most seductive creaminess, on the principle of innocent penny plain and naughty twopenny coloured, but perish the suggestion! What the gospel of austerity demands is tastelessness and insipidity and nothing that flatters the senses or the appetite can hope for an import licence. An American Professor named Rhine has proved by an interminable series of experiments with playing cards that the gift of precognition or prophecy is a fairly common human talent. I have an idea that a *Punch* artist was working on that faculty in 1894 and that the caption to his drawing was really the report of a conversation that was to take place fifty-four years later between a Minister of Food and his Under-Secretary of State: 'Botticelli isn't a wine, you Juggins! Botticelli's a cheese.'

Perhaps something of the same prophetic spirit may be traced in *Alice in Wonderland*, when Alice first sat down at the March Hare's tea party. ' "Have some wine," the March Hare said in an encouraging tone. Alice looked all round the table, but there was nothing on it but tea. "I don't see any wine," she remarked. "There isn't any," said

185

the March Hare. "Then it wasn't very civil of you to offer it," said Alice angrily.'

Quite inexcusably I shared Alice's indignation, when nearly thirty years ago I was attached to the Press retinue of the Prince of Wales on his visit to Canada and the United States. Prohibition was at its height. People came to visit the guests from overseas with newspaper-wrapped bottles under their arms, and the visitor underwent agonies of internal conflict between the fear of being poisoned with wood alcohol or some deadly concoction and the politeness that shrank from refusing the offer of a drink regarded by its donor as precious refreshment in a dry and stony land. Of course on that official tour there were banquets and toasts galore, and to look at the decorated tables with their array of wine glasses one might have supposed that for the moment the iron fetters of Prohibition would be relaxed. Alice looking round the table might have thought that the March Hare was asking her to choose between Sherry and a cocktail, Claret and Burgundy, Champagne and sparkling Burgundy, with Port or Brandy to follow. She would have seen plenty of glasses on the table, though never a bottle. Behind screens and curtains there was a certain activity; official visitors, royal and otherwise, might wet their whistles in guilty secrecy with something of which the teetotaller would not approve, but when it came to the feast, the nakedness of the land was bare. The soul- and stomach-chilling beverage, iced water, was varied with temperance fruit juices made to look like wine, and toasts were drunk in unfermented grape juice masquerading in a champagne glass. As the meal proceeded and the iced water got to work, conversation grew more and more frigid and forced, and when the orators were released the stillness of a polar winter descended on the tables where the gaps of empty seats steadily widened. Who could drink with feeling or sincerity a toast given in unfermented grape juice?

It was pathetic in those days how the generous host

wrestled with the bigotry of those who held the drinking of a glass of Claret a far more deadly sin than a breach of the seventh commandment, and who in defiance of the Greek language and common sense wished to make glad the hearts of the wedding guests at a marriage at Cana in Galilee with grape juice that had never been transfigured by the miracle of fermentation. One kindly friend took me to Greenwich Village where he paid enormous sums for what after all these years I can now confess was the worst bottle of Burgundy I ever tasted, and we swallowed down its nastiness in an atmosphere of dramatic secrecy that was as ridiculous as it was revolting. On another occasion when our hearts were to be softened towards the policy of Woodrow Wilson, which left the League of Nations disastrously suspended like Mahomet's coffin between heaven and earth, real sparkling Burgundy had been gathered for our entertainment with a lavishing of pains worthy of a better cause.

Disraeli's Mr. Mountchesney would have been in his element in New York in those Prohibition days. 'I rather like bad wine,' said Mr. Mountchesney in *Sybil*; 'one gets so bored with good wine.' Alas! today there is no need for Mr. Mountchesney to borrow the time machine and fly back into the past and cross the Atlantic to find a remedy for his boredom. The Golden Age, when good wine was like the grasshopper, a burden and desire for it failed, is very far away, and there has been no limit to the multitude of samples on which the student of bad wine and wine substitutes could train his palate to endurance and insensibility. *Sybil* was written in 1845, so that Mr. Mountchesney had had the Clarets of the 1811 Comet and Waterloo Port to bore him. A generation earlier, Jane Austen's Mr. Woodhouse, that valetudinarian, happy with an egg boiled very soft and a basin of nice smooth gruel, thin, but not too thin, no doubt eschewed wine both good and bad for his stomach's sake, but Mr. Weston had a good cellar. Emma was convinced that Mr. Elton had been drinking too much of Mr.

Weston's good wine when the vicar of Highbury began making love to her in the carriage, though he 'had only drunk wine enough to elevate his spirits, not at all to confuse his intellects.' To Mr. Woodhouse's credit be it remembered that he did ask Mrs. Goddard what she would say to *half* a glass of wine: 'A *small* half glass, put into a tumbler of water? I do not think it could disagree with you.'

It is a long step from Jane Austen to Richard Le Gallienne: I suppose the title of that novel of his *The Quest of the Golden Girl* was worth preserving; the editors of the Dictionary evidently think so, though they can hardly imagine that it will be read by the modern generation, for all its recommendation of great grapes and white wine as amorous food. Its author was precious enough, but I do not think that he ever indulged in a comparison so audacious as that which figures in a newly-published novel. A woman's throat is described as 'golden, the colour of some frail, sweet wine poured into a glass and held up to the light.' The reviewer criticized the word 'sweet' as otiose and that *fin gourmet*, Mr. Ambrose Heath, charged to the novelist's defence insisting that the adjective is essential to the description. 'There is all the difference,' he writes, 'between the rather chilly hue of a dry white wine, say a Chablis, and the pale golden warmth of a Sauternes.' Perhaps the epithet *sweet* is justified by the argument, though heaven knows that the dryest Montrachet may be warmly golden, but can the word *frail* be appropriately applied to Sauternes? In an Oxford Common Room the other day, I heard the gravest objection taken to the application of the word *clever* to wine, and the phrase *a clever little wine*, which I feel sure was erroneously attributed to the late Ernest Oldmeadow, seems to me to belong to the category of *the pale smile* and *the frail Sauternes*. A *frail* Sauternes sounds to me absurd; for what can be more robust than the extravagant richness of a Château Yquem? And it is scarcely fair to accuse any wine of moral frailty, the moral—or immoral—

frailty of a peccant beauty. *Frail* is certainly out of place, and I do not feel sure that I should fall enamoured of a lady with a golden throat, unless gold referred to the sounds it emitted like Sarah Bernhardt's *voix d'or* or the telephone Time girl's golden voice and not to the colour of the skin. Gold is the colour of the bilious and jaundiced. Carew's lady had a bird's nest in her throat so golden was her singing:

> Ask me no more whither doth haste
> The nightingale when May is past;
> For in your sweet dividing throat
> She winters and keeps warm her note.

But what Carew fancied was 'a rosy cheek' and 'a coral lip.'

A quotation from Crabbe about 'the poor toper whose untutor'd sense, sees bliss in ale and can with wine dispense,' reinforced by Benjamin Britten's opera *Peter Grimes* set me studying the works of that poet. What an inn the 'Queen Caroline' of the Borough had once been, and how hard to find its like today—as for its barmaid, not a hope!

> There fires inviting blazed, and all around
> Was heard the twinking bells' seducing sound;
> The nimble waiters to that sound from far
> Sprang to the call, then hasten'd to the bar;
> Where a grand priestess of the temple sway'd,
> The most obedient, and the most obey'd;
> Rosy and round, adorn'd in crimson vest,
> And flaming ribands at her ample breast . . .
> Her port in bottles stood, a well-stain'd row
> Drawn for the evening from the pipe below;
> Three powerful spirits fill'd a parted case,
> Some cordial bottles stood in secret place;
> Fair acid-fruits in nets above were seen,
> Her plate was splendid, and her glasses clean;
> Basins and bowls were ready on the stand,
> And measures clatter'd in her powerful hand.

The Lady of the Bar, the Paragon of Service, as queenly in her own line as Queen Victoria was to be in hers, serving port and punch, and brandy, rum and gin—(whisky had not yet found its way south) from a Tantalus, with netted lemons for the punch overhead, and everything as bright and polished as elbow grease could make it has been swallowed up in *the dark backward and abysm of time*. 'Bitter barmaid, waning fast,' apostrophized Tennyson in his *Vision of Sin*, but he was surely addressing himself to the wrong functionary when he told her: 'See that sheets are on my bed.'

In the earlier century to which Crabbe belonged, there was still a sense of fitness and hierarchical order: 'The gentle fair on nervous tea relied,' but

> Champagne the courtier drinks, the spleen to chase,
> The colonel Burgundy, and Port his Grace;
> Turtle and 'rrack the city rulers charm,
> Ale and content the labouring peasants warm.

These lines occur in a poem on *Inebriety*. Crabbe's father was a drunkard, and he had every reason to dwell on the virtues of moderation, but he always has a good word for the temperate use of wine.

> Wine like the rising sun possession gains,
> And drives the mist of dullness from the brains;
> The gloomy vapour from the spirit flies,
> And views of gaiety and gladness rise.

But in those days, the restraint of austerity as opposed to the limitation of poverty was unknown, and the night would end in fuddled Friendship weeping and jovial Folly sleeping.

> When wine no more o'erwhelms the labouring brain,
> But serves a gentle stimulus; we know
> How wit must sparkle and fancy flow.

Such was Crabbe's ideal, but unfortunately it was rarely reached or maintained in the Clubs at Aldborough, which inspired his Muse. There was the Book Club, where members ate and drank too much to *think or thoughts exchange*. There was no time for intercourse of mind, when each

dish was prepared with skill to invite and detain the struggling appetite, and then the wine went quickly round 'till
struggling Fancy was by Bacchus bound.' How in these days
our poet would have appreciated the high thinking and
plain living enforced by poverty on our nation! There
would be no danger of the feast of wisdom being interrupted
by the coarser pleasures of a banquet or the flow of soul
broken by the pouring of good wine. All his fellows cared
for were *primeurs, the earliest dainties and the oldest Port.*
Yet there were some vacant hours, *ere wine to folly
spurred the giddy guest*, that might have been devoted to
improving conversation, but would you believe it? the
dissipated club-men waste them by playing cards, whist in
fact.

> . . . groaning nations and contending kings
> Are all forgotten for these painted things:
> Paper and paste, vile figures and poor spots,
> Level all minds, philosophers and sots.

But the depths of eighteenth-century provincial degradation
are reached with a Tobacco Club almost comparable with
Dante's Inferno.

> A Club there is of SMOKERS—Dare you come
> To that close, clouded, hot, narcotic room?
> When, midnight past, the very candles seem
> Dying for air, and give a ghastly gleam;
> When curling fumes in lazy wreaths arise,
> And prosing topers rub their winking eyes;
> When the long tale, renew'd when last they met,
> Is spliced anew, and is unfinished yet.

The sordid horrors of an opium den could hardly be more
nauseating, and it is well that Crabbe did not live in an age
when tobacco is smoked in Duchess's drawing rooms.

191

VI

Calories and Christmas

WHAT is a calorie? A dictionary tells me that it is the amount of heat required to raise the temperature of one kilogramme of water one degree. How heartily our rulers patted themselves on the back when they announced the glad news that every member of the population had been every day raising the temperature of 3,000 kilogrammes one degree—or was it one kilogramme of water, 3,000 degrees?—and that consequently the ordinary British family had had about the best Christmas in living memory. It is nice to think of the entire British nation steaming away like boiling kettles and enjoying it as much as if they were tucking away, not into a microscopic Polish turkey all skin and bones, but into a gigantic pre-war bubbly jock accompanied by an unstinted abundance of Christmas fare. Yet I cannot help thinking that most of us could remember better Christmas rejoicings in the days when we did not trouble about calories and had no need to console ourselves for not getting just a little of what we fancy by trying to imagine that we are kettles boiling on the hob. As a water-heater I have no ambitions. It is conceivable that all this calorie business is no more than a smoke screen. I have a distinct recollection that in the days before the war scientists of the highest eminence proclaimed

192

that calories had become a hopelessly obsolete standard of measurement for nutrition, and that the only unit that counted was the vitamin. We might stuff ourselves with cálories *ad nauseam* and boil gallons of metaphorical water in the alembics of our bodies, and be not a scrap the better for it, since the only thing that counted was vitamins. Then the war came and calories were raised from the dead to pull wool over our eyes, because I presume the victims of official control would have seen through a vitamin ramp; for a vitamin is a slippery and elusive unit.

There was no thought of calories in Addison's mind when he wrote of Christmas at Sir Roger de Coverley's in No. 269 of *The Spectator*, dated January 8, 1711–12. That very morning he tells us he had been knocked up by the coachman of his worthy friend Sir Roger, and invited to take a turn with his master in Gray's-inn walks. Evidently the visit was an early one, and it would seem that the matutinal manifestations of catarrh, nowadays invariably put down to *Pellegrini's deadly tube*, otherwise the cigarette, were no less widespread in the days of the clay church-warden, centuries before the cigarette was even thought of. For Addison writes that he had no sooner come into Gray's-inn walks but he heard his friend upon the terrace "hemming twice or thrice to himself with great vigour, for he loves to clear his pipes in good air (to make use of his own phrase), and is not a little pleased with anyone who takes notice of the strength which he still employs in his morning hems.'

Sir Roger fell into an account of the diversions which had passed in his house during the holidays. The reader will remember that the date is January 8th, two hundred and forty years ago. Sir Roger followed the laudable custom of his ancestors in always keeping open house at Christmas. What would his generous soul have done in these days of Food Ministers with their points, coupons and controls? I fear it might have tempted him into breaking the law. He, however, lucky man, was free to kill eight fat hogs for the season, to deal about his chines very liberally among his neighbours, and to send a string of hog's-puddings with a pack of cards to every poor family in the parish.

'I have often thought,' says Sir Roger, 'it happens very well that Christmas should fall out in the middle of winter. It is the most dead, uncomfortable time of the year, when the poor people would suffer very much from their poverty and cold, if they had not good cheer, warm fires, and Christmas gambols to support them. I love to rejoice their hearts at this season, and to see the whole village merry in my great hall. I allow a double quantity of malt to my small beer, and set it a-running for twelve days to everyone that calls for it. I have always a piece of cold beef and a mince-pye on the table, and am wonderfully pleased to see my tenants pass away a whole evening in playing their innocent tricks and smutting one another.'

Smutting presumably means *chaffing*, and it is easy for the mind's eye to conjure up a picture of the benevolent Sir Roger—is his dance ever danced nowadays?—presiding over the Christmas merry-making with a fatherly simplicity which was in Addison's time already becoming old-fashioned, not to say primitive. He heads his paper with a quotation, *aevo rarissima nostra simplicitas—simplicity most rare in our days*—which as it comes from Ovid's *Ars Amatoria* may have had originally a less innocent intention than it sounds, though I have no text handy to check the reference.

Who could find an equation in calories to express the good cheer of a Dickens' Christmas? Scrooge had his vision of *Christmas Present*. 'Heaped up on the floor were turkeys, geese, game, poultry, brawn, great joints of meat, sucking-pigs, long wreaths of sausages, mince-pies, plum-puddings, barrels of oysters, red-hot chestnuts, cherry-cheeked apples, juicy oranges, luscious pears, immense twelfth-cakes, and seething bowls of punch that made the chamber dim with their delicious steam.'

Equally incalculable were the calories of the Dingley Dell festivities. They started on December 22nd, when we are told that 'Long after the ladies had retired, did the hot elder wine, well qualified with brandy and spice, go round, and round and round again, and sound was the sleep and pleasant were the dreams that followed.' It is provoking not to be told what wine or wines were drunk in the innumerable toasts at the wedding breakfast next morning, but the supply of calories must have been phenomenal. It will be remembered that everyone toasted everyone else, that the poor relations who were presumably not accustomed to such potations disappeared mysteriously under the table, but their effect on other members of the party was even more extra-ordinary. It sent out all the males on 'a five-and-twenty mile walk, undertaken at Wardle's recommendation to get rid of the effects of the wine at breakfast.' Truly there were giants in the earth in those days! Mr. Pickwick, after all those toasts, walked twenty-five miles, ate a hearty dinner with more toasts, and then danced with a vigour that nothing could stop—no, not if the house had been on fire —except the cessation of the music. The Portuguese grape-gatherers who work all day and dance all night have some claim to the title of indefatigable, but the portly middle-aged founder of the Pickwick Club seems to have outdone them. I'm afraid the novelist must have made a mistake about the distance; surely a short-lived December day could scarcely allow time for a wedding breakfast and a twenty-five mile walk?

Robert Charvay turned Pickwick into a French play which was put on at the Vaudeville Theatre in Paris, and I had a good deal of fun in helping him work out the festivities at Dingley Dell. The scene was a good repro-duction of an old English farm kitchen with a table groaning with turkeys, geese, barons of beef, plum puddings and mince pies of the theatrical variety. The *clou* of the evening was unquestionably the Snapdragon; on the night of the

195

Répétition Générale it was a real dish of flaming brandy from which the actors snatched real raisins and really burnt their fingers at what seemed to me the imminent risk of setting the theatre afire. The Parisian accepted it as one of those exotic whimsical oddities that always tickle his fancy. I went to some trouble to find a recipe for the wassail, a mighty bowl of which, 'something smaller than an ordinary washhouse copper,' circulated for the rest of the evening. Unfortunately there seemed no way of getting its local colour across the foot-lights, and steaming hot water in the end masqueraded as that warming and cheerful compound of our forefathers.

It can only have been the obsession of calories which set me dreaming on Christmas night in the days of austerity of Yuletide at Dotheboys Hall. I found myself in a bare and dirty room filled with lean and hungry boys and I knew I was in the schoolroom of Dotheboys Hall. Standing at a desk was a formidable lady; one could safely say that there was no nonsense about her. Though she had features that vaguely recalled to me one of our rulers of today, she was clad in the costume of Mrs. Squeers, with a dimity night jacket, her hair in papers, and a bonnet perched on the top of a night cap which was held in place by a yellow kerchief tied under her masculine chin. On a desk before her, there stood an immense basin from which she was ladling some liquid in a gigantic wooden spoon and pouring it down the throats of her unwilling pupils.

'Please,' said a pathetic, quavering voice, 'please, surely not brimstone and treacle on Christmas Day.'

'Nonsense,' came the uncompromising reply, 'you must have brimstone and treacle, because their calories spoil your appetites and comes cheaper than breakfast and dinner. It is just snobbery not to like brimstone and treacle better than bacon and eggs. Look at our vital statistics. The new feeding habits which we are establishing will make you all live ever so much longer.'

From another desk there came the voice of a man with a cane whom I recognized at once as the Rt. Hon. Mr. Squeers. 'Conquer your passions, boys, and don't be eager after vittles. Subdue your appetites, my dears, and you've conquered human natur'.'

Mrs. Squeers took up the tale, as she gave an extra large dollop of the inexpensive and nauseous mixture to young Mobbs who, it will be remembered, would not eat fat and turned up his nose at cow's liver broth. 'Until the nineteenth century, no one ever thought of eating eggs and bacon for breakfast, and now we know that a large breakfast for an average man is a crime against his own body.'

At this point to my amazement I found myself breaking into the conversation. 'How right you are!' I cried. 'You, Mrs. Squeers, must have been reading *The Times* leader on *Petit Déjeuner*. Let us "resist the blandishments of bacon, the charms (now noticeably faded) of the sausage." Yours is the glory that today we do not even dream of those succulent and deadly temptations which the leader writer so eloquently enumerates. "Devilled grouse wantonly superimposed on kedgeree, kidneys and bacon following the porridge in its facile descent, fish-cakes the size of billiard balls, above all the two or three slices of ham which so often, so dreadfully often, rounded off the criminal proceedings." '

'The very thought of such gluttony,' cried Mrs. Squeers, 'belongs to a chronic dyspeptic and you must have a double dose.'

She descended upon me with a brimming spoon, but somehow I evaded her charge and, as is the way of dreams, everything went on as if I was not there. Physicking was over and the Rt. Hon. Mr. Squeers was standing at a huge table covered with Christmas fare.

'You are good boys,' he said, 'and have taken your physic well. Just look at all the beautiful things the Government has collected for your Christmas fare. There is only one principle on which we must insist; everybody must have

197

exactly the same share of exactly the same delicacies as everybody else. To begin with, here is some magnificent wine such as has not been offered to you since the war. Claret and Burgundy of rare vintages, senatorial Port, noble brandy.' We all crowded round the table reaching out our hands for the bottles, but suddenly they were whisked away.

'Pantisocracy,' he said, 'forbids. Away with all these bottles! Now I have counted your heads, I see there is not enough to go round evenly. Much better do without than feel that someone has something that you have not. That is what is called charity.'

'It is only social prejudice,' said Mrs. Squeers, 'that makes people crave after fashionable wines. If they did not want to pretend that they were better than they are, they would be content with ordinary beverages, Algerian wine for instance. Look, here we have thousands of bottles of it, plenty to go round and leave some over, and it will not cost you more than seven shillings a bottle.'

'No, my dear,' said Mr. Squeers, 'they cannot have that Algerian wine, as it has all been sold to Germany.'

'What on earth,' I asked, 'is Germany going to do with it?'

'That is not our concern, since you all ought to be as jolly as sandboys on Adam's ale. Our Chancellor drinks nothing else and you can think yourselves very lucky that he has not put a tax on it.'

Piles of luxuries were now to be seen on the Ministry table, caviare, *pâté de foie gras* and every rarity, but they all disappeared one after the other, because it was quite impossible to share them out equally between the whole population. There were protests that one person liked one thing and another another, that one person needed more to eat than another, that in fact an identical diet for an infinite variety of digestions and palates was not so scientifically praiseworthy as it sounded. Mr. Squeers replied that it was the policy to reduce all tastes, stomachs and minds to a single uniform standard, so that a mass-produced nation might be able to masticate the blessings of mass-production.

Mrs. Squeers grew particularly eloquent, when someone ventured to murmur that what he would like for his Christmas was a nice big juicy steak. 'Fie upon you!' she cried. 'In a classless society no one would ever think of wanting steaks. You were taught when you were young that the wealthy ate steaks and that it was the thing to do, like wearing a white stiff collar or having frequent baths. What you really like, let me tell you, is a nice portion of dog fish or a collop of conger eel. You do not really like salmon or Dover soles; it is only fashion and imitation that makes you think of them; herrings are far nicer and their food content superior.'

A voice murmured in protest 'just a little of what you fancy.'

'*Fancy*, that is just the trouble. All a matter of social imputation. If all the peerage ate snoek, we should not be able to keep pace with the demand, and as for whale, if people knew that it was served at the Mansion House as a substitute for turtle soup, they would have to impose new controls on the whale fisheries. Look at cheese. Here at Dotheboys Hall we countenance nothing but good honest soaplike mouse-trap, because it is all the same. It is as shameful to hanker after green cheese and blue cheese and all the naughty coloured sophisticated varieties as it is to yearn after green carnations, black tulips, and all the nameless perversions for which they stand. Only an eccentric would dote on Wensleydale or Stilton, and Blue Vinney, Cheshire and Cheddar as they are sent forth from their native places bearing the stamp of Deadly Sins. We have done our best to preserve our shores from the deadly infection of Roquefort, Camembert, Brie, Gorgonzola and the other curses of foreign caseous origin, but these foreigners are difficult to deal with. At least we can prevent the English from eating their own more sophisticated

199

cheeses and give them virtuous Transoceanic mouse-trap for their daily ration. The day may yet come, when in no country will it be possible to buy the cheese that is made in it. You will be able to buy Stilton and the rest on the Continent and in America, while the cheeses of France and Italy will have this country as their exclusive market, if really we are compelled to import any of these immoral cheeses.'

At this point Mr. Squeers wheeled in a noble carving table after the manner of those that once were wont to enthrone the lordly joints from which portions were cut to stay the hunger of the City magnate.

'Here,' he proclaimed, laying his hand in the polished silver cover, 'is our *pièce de résistance*, such a glorious dish for Christmas as the world has never seen. This vegetarian tit-bit will compensate over and over again for shortage of turkeys, geese, plum puddings, mince-pies, and all the unwholesome foods which once encouraged Christmas indigestion. It is part of what Mrs. Squeers calls so well our new feeding habits, that refinement of the Art of Good Living which owes its origin to our Government.'

At this point I was attacked by a desire to be rude and most inexcusably ejaculated an impolite monosyllable: 'Nuts!'

Mr. Squeers took up the word at once: 'Nuts, it is ground-nuts and the most expensive and delectable dish ever offered to a nation for its Christmas fare.'

As he spoke he removed the cover with a flourish and hands were stretched out eagerly to grasp anything edible that the dream Barmecide's feast might offer to the would-be Christmas merry-maker. Mr. Squeers burst into poetry in the highest heroic vein, as he pointed to a huge platter,

A table richly spread in regal mode,
With dishes piled, and meats of noblest sort
And savour; beasts of chase, or fowl of game,
In pastry built, or from the spit, or boiled,
Gris-amber-steamed; all fish from sea or shore . . .

Mr. Squeers might have continued his quotation from *Paradise Regained*, with its description of the banquet provided by Satan for a temptation in the wilderness, but he was checked by the general cry, 'There is nothing there.' And indeed to my dreaming eyes it seemed that the cover had been removed from an empty dish. The ground-nuts were like the Emperor's clothes, non-existent, though how incomparably expensive!

So I awoke from a vision of Squeersian austerity. *Sursum corda!* Awake we can escape from the controlled nonsense and enjoy ourselves, if frugally, yet with a contented mind and a contented palate, that organ which scientists and politicians vie with one another in torturing. I stumbled on a quotation from Charles Lamb which seemed peculiarly apposite in the circumstances of the case. 'Old Christmas is a-coming to the confusion of Puritans, Muggletonians, Anabaptists, Quakers, and that unwassailing Crew. He cometh not with his wonted gait, he is shrunk nine inches in his girth, but is yet a lusty follow.'

Yes, our Christmas in these years of grace is indeed shrunk in girth. There is no Sir Roger de Coverley left in the land to kill eight fat hogs for the season and deal chines and hog's puddings liberally about among his neighbours, to say nothing of keeping open house for twelve days with beer brewed specially strong and a piece of cold beef and a mince-pie on the table for anyone who calls. Yet my experience as the Hon. Sec. of a Pig Club tells me that there will be quite a few worthy folk who will be killing a pig this Yuletide, perhaps on December 21st, of which we are told

> The day of Saint Thomas, the blessed Divine,
> Is good for brewing, baking, and killing fat swine.

Elizabeth Lucas who quotes this rhyme in her delightful *Good Year*, goes on to make her readers' mouths water by quoting from Charles Lamb's immortal *Dissertation upon Roast Pig*. 'There is no flavour comparable, I will contend,

201

to that of the crisp, tawny, well-matched, not over-roasted *crackling*, as it is well called—the very teeth are invited to their share of the pleasure at this banquet in overcoming the coy, brittle resistance—with the adhesive oleaginous— oh, call it not fat! but an indefinable sweetness growing up to it—the tender blossoming of fat—fat cropped in the bud —taken in the shoot—in the first innocence—the cream and quintessence of the child pig's yet pure food—the lean, no lean, but a kind of animal manna—or rather, fat and lean (if it must be so) so blended and running into each other, that both together make but one ambrosian result, or common substance.'

There is a recommendation of the thirteenth-century Physicians of Myddvai, which it may still be within our power to follow. 'If you would be at all times merry, eat saffron in meat and drink and you will never be sad: but beware of eating over-much, lest you should die of excessive joy.' Where saffron comes from I do not know, but I am pretty sure that it is not derived from the dollar countries. Since it is the produce of the crocus, home-grown saffron may be within the bounds of possibility, and I would humbly suggest the encouragement of crocus as a simple non-inflationary means of making the heart glad.

Failing saffron, we may follow William Caxton's advice: 'At Crystmasse and at Ester, man ought to vysit and see his good frende.' Our journeys should be safe from bad weather at this season, for the period of Halcyon Days endures from December 15th to 30th and during this fortnight, while the kingfisher is breeding, the wisdom of the ancients guarantees a perfectly calm sea. Travelling thus in fine weather, we may be guided in our visits by our knowledge of the good cheer we are likely to find. We may have to travel far afield, if we are to fare the best, supposing that there is any truth in the dictum of one of our French visitors. 'English cooking at its best is the most delicate and wholesome in the world. What a pity that so many streets lie between the houses where it is to be found at its best.'

St. Francis tells us that in memory of the stable at Bethlehem, everyone who has an ox or an ass shall on Christmas Eve provide them with the best he can. In the country it is a night of miracles, this *Réveillon*, which in towns can only be celebrated with prosaic junketings, apart from the one midnight mass in the Church ritual. No creature sleeps except the serpent. The ox and ass converse in human speech. The cock, the trumpet to the morn, summons the sun throughout the hours of darkness.

> The bird of dawning singeth all night long;
> And then, they say, no spirit can walk abroad;
> The nights are wholesome.

At this blessed time Bees sing in their hives. There is no end to the glimpses of the unseen world that Christmas may offer to the romantic, and those of a frivolous turn of mind may take the opportunity of reading Saki Munro's short story 'Bertie's Christmas Eve.' There they will learn how the Steffink family emulating the Russian peasant went out to the cow-house to hear the cows talking and were locked in by the undesirable nephew Bertie, who proceeded to wassail with other undesirables on the good things provided for the party.

It was thoughtful of the Food Ministry to choose Christmastime for the feeding of our gaiety with the invention of the Sherry Cow in default of calories and turkeys. This fabulous quadruped became involved with the Rubá'iyát of Omar Khayyám in the doggerel churned up by laughter.

> A Book of Verses underneath the Bough,
> A Jug of Wine milk'd from the Sherry Cow—
> And Thou beside me in the Wilderness . . .

Who could that mysterious *Thou* be, *the fair, the chaste, and unexpressive she*? The unnamed Milkmaid of the Sherry Cow? Surely not the then reigning Ministress of Food? No, the rhyme of my delirium went off the lines.

Our National Dairy-Maid Summersilk
Was skimming the Cream from the Bristol Milk.

Doubtless she made it into honest mouse-trap cheese or churned it into better-than-butter margarine.

It really seems worth putting on record the surprising fact that the birthplace of the Sherry Cow was to be found not in the land of the Pobble and Aunt Jobiska's Runcible Cat with the crimson whiskers, but in Whitehall. It was born in a moment of tragedy. The virginal conscience of the 'Food Standards and Labelling Division,' the Round Table of Mr. Strachey's Food Ministry, suffused the cheeks of all its Knights with blushes of ingenuous horror at the moral turpitude of a label submitted for their sanction. It was all the worse that it had been in use for a century or two without shocking anyone. BRISTOL MILK! A manifest contravention of Regulation 1 of the Defence (Sale of Food) Regulations! BRISTOL MILK! howled the stricken bureaucrats—the words indicated the presence of milk, and as such suggested that the wine had certain special nutritive qualities. The nurse who went out to buy Bristol Milk for the babe in arms would be as abominably cheated as that nurse of Gilbert's who so unfortunately apprenticed her charge to a pirate instead of to a pilot. What defence could we hope to have against the Atom Bomb if a label misled a nurse 'as to the nature, substance, or quality of a food or in particular as to its nutritional or dietary value,' and set her feeding her babies on Bristol Milk with Bristol Cream for a treat? How exhilarating it would be to the unrighteous to see dozens of Sherry bottles taking the place of the milk bottles so generously showered down on our schools!

It was interesting to observe that our officials—how unkind of Messrs. John Harvey to tell them that no one but an imbecile could connect their Sherry with the product of a cow—seemed to regret the absence of cow's

204

milk in the wine, taking up an attitude utterly opposed to that of Sir John Falstaff, who, one suspects, knew a great deal more about Sack than our modern Palladium of Purity about wine. The reader will remember how after his lamentable ducking in the Thames in a dirty clothes basket, he called for no mere chalices of Sack, but a pottle—that is two quarts—brewed finely, and when Bardolph asked him whether he would have it brewed with eggs, he replied: 'Simple of itself; I'll have no pullet sperm in my brewage.' Falstaff would have no farm produce in his Sherry, and I think he was right.

There was a delightfully humourless reasonableness about the communication in which the Ministry replied to the argument that if Bristol Cream must go the same way as Bristol Milk, as logically it must, there would have to be at the same time a wholesale massacre of shaving creams, hair creams, face creams, boot creams, and all other creams, which can claim no lacteal provenance. It remarks so patiently as though it were dealing with a foolish child that it is 'discussing regulations pertaining to the sale of food only.' I feel that we all ought to help our rulers in this crusade against the deceptive appellation. Have they thought of the Welsh Rarebit, which I have often seen written on menus with unpardonable duplicity, Welsh Rabbit? Then the Scotch Woodcock should attract their immediate attention. By this time some misguided canner of food must have enclosed a Scotch Woodcock in a tin and put a label on it. What a chance for a prosecution! The criminal would be driven to confess that there is no more woodcock, Scottish or otherwise, in a Scotch Woodcock than there is turtle in Mock Turtle Soup. There again most clearly is an opening for instant Ministerial action. What could be more calculated to deceive than the suggestion that it is possible to trace a connection between a turtle and a calf's head? Again something might be done about Charlotte Russe. I doubt very much whether there is any

Charlotte in the case, and even if there is, I do not believe that she comes from the other side of the Iron Curtain. Most unpardonable of all are offences against childish innocence, and in these days when the future generation is so much more important than the present it is heart-breaking to think that with all our safeguards and controls there is not a single one to protect the schoolchild's pennies. If the coming generation asks for bulls'-eyes, it wants bulls'-eyes, should be given bulls'-eyes for its pennies, and the law should see to it that only taurine optics, and not mere peppermint substitutes, should be sold as bulls'-eyes.

To be serious for a moment, when all is said and done, it is disquieting to think that there is someone wandering about the world, who wrote the letters about Bristol Milk. They may make for gaiety, but the writing of them would surely provide a valid defence against almost any charge from black market to black murder. 'Gentlemen of the jury, my client suffered from the delusion that Sherry should be milked from a cow. How could he be expected to know what he was doing when he killed a pig without getting a licence—or when he cut Mr. So and So's throat.' Any verdict of guilty could only be qualified by insane.

An Epilogue
on
Wine Tomorrow

Conscience Professionnelle and a Wine
Union of Western Europe

THANKLESS is the task of the prophet, unless he
cautiously confines himself to long-term predictions
outside the range of our mortal span; yet this book
can hardly be brought to a fitting conclusion without a few
words about the wines of tomorrow and the wine-lover's
prospects in the immediate future. His well-being depends
on the answers that time will give to two questions of fact:
will good wine still be made and offered for sale, and if it
is, will the English wine-lover be allowed to have it?

It is easier to answer the first question than the second.
A few months ago I went to France for such time as the
Treasury would permit with the express object of discovering
whether the spirit of integrity, which is as essential as the
juice of the grape to the making of great wine and which
made the French peasant the bedrock foundation of the
French nation, had survived the dissolving agonies of
defeat and occupation. It was not from the world-famous
wine-districts that I expected to obtain enlightenment; for
it is difficult to see behind the screen of routine and
sophistication where production is on a considerable scale
and is directed towards the satisfaction of world markets,
which so often lack discernment. I thought it easier to
address my inquiries to the small *vigneron*, the humble
local wine-grower with a few acres of vineyard in a region

where wine is made for home consumption. He might safely be taken as a representative French peasant and I had no doubt—indeed I knew from past experience—that a common love of wine would put us on terms of confidence in the twinkling of an eye. Such men make wines as an artist paints a picture or a poet pens a poem, not for fame or profit, but for their friends' approval, their own enjoyment, and the satisfaction of their own conceit. In days gone by they had been guided by the spirit of *conscience professionnelle*, the conscientious integrity of purpose, which eschewed the easy short cuts that may mean commercial success and followed the hard, long way round of care and toil which leads to quality and small profit and, be it added, personal satisfaction. In the last issue, the production of a great wine depends on the humility of its maker, who must start with the recognition that human Science may be the handmaid, but can never be the mistress, of Nature, alike in the vineyard and the world.

My voyage of exploration carried me first to Touraine, rather too renowned a wine district for my purpose, but I was happy to renew acquaintance with those red wines of Bourgeuil and Chinon that Rabelais loved. I found them distinctly bigger and more fragrant with their special raspberry scent than I remembered, and took a pleasure in the thought that on the Loire the vines of Bordeaux and Burgundy meet, so that a perfect red Loire wine should combine the virtues of both. I must, I fear, admit that so far I have failed to meet that ideal combination: for I have never tasted either Joué or Saint Avertin, those neighbours of Tours made from mingled *pinot* and *cabernet*, which are locally said to stand comparison with either a fine Burgundy or fine Claret.

Touraine, however, is essentially a country of white wines. Rabelais' *taffeta* wine, wine soft as silk, from the Clos de la Devinière at Chinon, was white. Few wines have suffered more from the flattery of imitation and from

210

rebellion against the ordinances laid down by Nature than Vouvray, and I was pleased to find some pleasant, natural wines, *sec*, *demi-sec*, or *moelleux* as the year dictated, with the Vouvray label, at the Family Hotel, Langeais, where I made my first stop. The proprietor, M. Cuigny, an admirable chef whose speciality it is to metamorphose the repulsive-looking crayfish he keeps in his fountain into attractive and appetizing delicacies, shared my interest in the conscientious rectitude of the wine-grower, and assured me that I should get a better insight into the local methods of wine-making at Montlouis than at Vouvray, as there everything was on a smaller scale.

Montlouis lies on the left bank of the Loire opposite Vouvray, and the aspect of its vineyards is much the same. The nice white wines it grows owe the charm of their freshness and fragrance to a complete lack of sophistication. The grapes are pressed slowly and, as soon as the boisterous fermentation is over, the wine is racked and bottled, the conditions of the vintage giving it its character and quality. To begin with, it may show like Vouvray a slight sparkle, but I was assured that this faint secondary fermentation passed very quickly, and I certainly did not see a Montlouis that was not still and bright.

M. Cuigny had given me an introduction to M. Henri Moreau, Propriétaire Viticulteur, and I found in him the very prophet of *conscience professionnelle*, one who enunciated with eloquence the fundamental principles which have directed the making of good wine since the days of Noah. A *vigneron* worthy of the name could only work with, and never against, Nature. Nature dictated the quality of each vintage, and it was as stupid as it was immoral to try to correct faults of the season by admixture of cane-sugar or alcohol and the other chemical expedients which reduce wine to the level of a manufactured composition. He had the true connoisseur's love for subtle shades of distinction and the charm of variety. He kept

211

each cask of his wine separate, so that each might develop its special individual qualities and that there might not be that cancelling out of attractive idiosyncrasies which is the inevitable result of blending.

The principles of the conscientious artist in wine, which M. Moreau set out as we discussed his wine, were repeated to me in similar circumstances by countless growers, and it would be tedious to reiterate their professions of devotion to the creed of all who find in wine aesthetic satisfaction. Of course, there were bottles that sought to compensate for the inferiority of their contents by the garish brilliance of their labels, but as a rule the local wines, white, pink, and red, were made conscientiously and with a minimum of sophistication. My itinerary carried me through Périgord, where I expected to learn more about truffles than wine, but it was on the boundary of that land of Cockaigne that I made my most interesting discovery and was introduced to a miracle worked by the strictest and most patient attention to the principles of the art of wine-making. The wines of Cahors are black and coarse and strong, commercial productions only useful for giving colour, substance, and strength to anaemic, tasteless, and feeble wines in cheap mass-production blends. There was a time when some wines of quality were made in this district, but they were consumed by their producers as the perfect accompaniment of the truffles of Périgord, and their secret which entailed the combination of a number of different grapes has been lost. At Sarlat I experimented with some wine labelled Vieux Cahors and found it not unlike that *omnium gatherum* of cheap rough wines called *pinard* in the first World War, but not so palatable.

At Roc-amadour, in the same Department of the Lot, I expressed my regret to the obliging Manager of the Hôtel du Lion d'Or that there were no local wines of account in his neighbourhood. He replied by pointing to two entries in his wine list, Château de Bonnecoste 1937 *rouge*, 350 francs; Château de Bonnecoste 1938 *blanc*, 400 francs.

'You must certainly see M. Brossier,' he said. 'Château de Bonnecoste is entirely his own creation and it is the only fine wine grown in the whole Department of the Lot.'

I tried both the red and the white Bonnecoste that day, and the red was a revelation. The wine of the 1937 vintage had some kinship with a Saint Emilion of quality, but it was darker, fuller-bodied, and combined with an aristocratic bouquet that velvety texture that one is wont to associate with great Burgundy. Its distinctive feature was the attractive grape flavour, faintly perceptible in certain years of Château Margaux, and conspicuous in the red Loire wines of Chinon and Bourgeuil which seem to me to lack the breed of Bonnecoste. It is often described by reference to the scent of a raspberry; munch a raspberry and at the same time smell a violet and the resultant taste-smell will approximate to it, though in the wine it is more subtle and refined.

Next day I drove some twenty miles to the Domaine de Bonnecoste, the home of this interesting wine, situated on a lonely plateau in the commune of Calès. M. Brossier, warned by telephone, was awaiting me and after completing the formality of selling a cow seemed as pleased to show me his wines as a painter to display his pictures to an art-lover. His domain consists of 1,500 acres, much of it rocky and picturesque with the source of a stream and the gorge through which it flows. Only 25 acres are under vines; for M. Brossier works in his vineyard, makes his wines, matures them, bottles them, and markets them almost single-handed, apart from family assistance. The imposing ruins of a medieval castle provide him with commodious cellars guarded from all changes of temperature by immense masses of masonry.

An official Report upon his vineyard and wines, drawn up by the Director of the Agricultural Services of the

Department, bears witness to M. Brossier's unique accomplishment. The vineyard was planted some forty or so years ago on very poor soil of chalky clay, and M. Brossier has patiently pursued for many years the experiment that is only now attaining its full measure of success. There are no vines on his land other than those noble plants on which the renown of the greatest Clarets and Sauternes depends; for red wines, *cabernet*, *merlot*, and *cot rouge* or *malbec*, and for white wines the melodiously named trio, *semillon*, *sauvignon*, *muscadelle*. Untiring perseverance in a system of trial and error has brought into being a wine worthy of a connoisseur's attention, and M. Brossier is officially recognized as the only wine-grower in the Department whose produce ranks with that of renowned vineyards.

Encouraged by this official approbation of M. Brossier's enterprise, I followed him under a scorching sun, with the cicadas singing madly, by a rough rocky path to the vaults where his wines were stored. On the way behind a low stone wall I noticed a plantation of young oak trees and made some remark about it.

'They are planted for the truffles,' said M. Brossier, and at the word *truffles* I pricked up my ears. My mind wandered from our immediate object, the wine of Bonnecoste, and stopping I beguiled my guide into conversation about this seductive delicacy.

Brillat-Savarin says that the truffle did not become fashionable until the beginning of the eighteenth century, when it became a perfect craze, and the title he bestowed upon it, *le diamant de la cuisine*, has become a cliché. Reference, however, is rarely made to the motive underlying the Prince of Gourmets' disquisition on *the diamond of the kitchen*. It mainly consists of an investigation—*un peu scabreuse peut-être*—into its alleged virtue as *amorous food*, if one may transfer to a fungus the phrase delicately applied by Richard Le Gallienne to *wine and great grapes*. The conclusion of the inquiry is discreetly expressed in the

214

following words: 'La truffe peut, en certaines occasions, rendre les femmes plus tendres et les hommes plus aimables.'

Be that as it may, the truffle is a curious and fascinating comestible, and I listened to what M. Brossier had to say about it with close attention. Very little seems to be known about its habits. No one has succeeded in cultivating it, but oak trees are planted in the pious hope, sometimes fulfilled, that the mycelium of the truffle—it has spawn like a mushroom—may form on the oak leaves, as the oak appears to have a special attraction for it. The spores, it is supposed, fall to the ground, and there develops just below the surface of the ground the black tuber which is the gourmet's delight. Its perfume can be scented by a dog or pig fifty yards away, and they share the gourmet's affection for the truffle. A black and white bitch of doubtful breed which accompanied us was an expert truffle hunter. Let her wind but the whiff of a truffle and she was off like a greyhound coursing a hare. Yet when she had run the fungus to earth, she had been trained not to dig for it, but to stand with one foot planted on the spot under which her nose told her the truffle was hiding, until her master came up and scooped it out, rewarding her with some titbit. Sows—the fair sex seems to have the keener scent for this tuber of Venus—are also employed, and they proceed at once to root out the kitchen diamond. They are taught to carry it to their master in their snout as delicately as a good game dog retrieves a bird, but sometimes the temptation is too great. There is a jerk and twist of the sow's head shooting the truffle down her gullet; we will draw a veil over the reception that awaits her from her owner.

The foundations of the castle provide M. Brossier with a number of scattered wine vaults, and in the old Guard Room with its ceiling supported by fine walnut beams— it is the best preserved part of the Château—he arrayed for my inspection as of a Guard of Honour five bottles of his wine and a bottle of his Brandy. The white wine outnumbered the red by four to one, but it was the red Bonnecoste of 1928 that interested me. Even after I had learned so much about M. Brossier and tasted the red wine of 1937, it came to me as a startling surprise. There are few of the finer growths of Claret, of which I have not tried at least one specimen of the 1928 vintage; much was expected of it, but to this day pretty well all of those wines remain dumb, hard, and generally disappointing. Not one of them has come up to expectation. · The Bonnecoste 1928 was exactly what we had hoped that the 1928 Clarets would be, when they were ripe in full maturity. It had all the good qualities I had observed in the 1937 the night before, raised to a higher power and harmonized by time. Its bouquet was delightfully delicate and flowery, its softness saved from any suspicion of mawkishness by a refreshing touch of acid, and the sweetness of its after-taste promised even longer life and a higher degree of excellence.

I asked M. Brossier how he had performed this miracle of producing on the most unpromising of sites with a tiny isolated vineyard a wine that might bear comparison with wines of the best report. He was at one with M. Moreau in submission to the rulings of Nature and antipathy to chemical expedients. His main discovery after years of patient research was that his wines, naturally partaking to some extent in the rough coarseness of the ordinary Cahors wines, had a great quantity of superfluities and waste products to get rid of in the lees, before they could claim to be wines of quality. Their maturing had to be long and thorough, and therefore as slow as possible. M. Brossier owed to Pasteur the knowledge that the development of a wine in the wood is conditioned by the amount of oxygen it takes up through the staves of the cask. In a small cask the operation is accelerated, since the surface of the wine against the staves and therefore more or less in contact with the outer air is greater in proportion to the contents of the barrel than it is in a larger receptacle. M. Brossier slows down the process by maturing his red wine in *muids* and *demi-muids*, casks of larger capacity than the *barrique* or hogshead of Bordeaux, so that the oxygen takes much longer to permeate their contents, and he is able to keep the wine improving in the wood year after year, until every trace of impurity has been shed to the satisfaction of his fastidious taste—which he finds a safer guide than any chemical analysis. His guiding principles are experiment and patience; thanks to them there is a general demand for his wines in all the best hotels of the region, thanks to them, he is able to enlarge his vineyard, and hand on to his sons a fine tradition.

I came back from France convinced that the art of wine-making was very much alive and that there was every hope that good wine would continue to be made so long as our civilization held together. There remained the question whether the inhabitants of these islands would be allowed to have his share of the enjoyment created by the *conscience professionnelle* of the continental *vigneron*. We are cut off from our neighbours by the estranging Channel and an almost impenetrable wall of customs duties. The width of the Channel has almost vanished, but the wall has never before been so thick and forbidding. Yet it seemed to me that never before had French and English been so nearly at one. Again and again I was deeply touched by the tribute of gratitude paid to an Englishman, because his country had kept the flag flying when all seemed lost.

It seemed inconceivable that our two nations should be held apart indefinitely by artificial barriers which made the estranging formalities of the past seem perfect freedom. If Churchill's gesture had borne fruit, his offer in the black hour of despair to make France and Britain one, there must have been an end to frontier red-tape, currency restrictions and customs walls. The union of Western Europe becomes

217

more and more a matter of vital urgency, and what better link could there be than wine. It is more than enough to have one Iron Curtain, such a poor substitute for the theatrical Safety Curtain, cleaving the Continent, and indeed the world, asunder; it is madness to multiply compartments and divisions. Our fortunes are bound up with those of France, and the prosperity which can alone restore our neighbours to their pristine power of defence depends to a great extent on their being able to send their wines abroad, unhampered by prohibitive tariffs. Actually the total revenue brought in by the crushing duties on wine represents scarcely a drop in the bottomless bucket of our Budget expenditure.

And France is not the only country that might be called into a Union with the exchange of wine as one of its basic principles. The wine trades of many countries have centred for hundreds of years round the British market, and the vineyards of Spain and Portugal as well as those of France would not have been what they are today without the custom of our country. On my return from France, I was invited by my old friends the Sandemans to visit their Bodegas in Jerez and their Lodges at Oporto to revise what I had written about Port and Sherry in the long ago, and their invitation gave me an opportunity to see for myself how far the wine-growers of Spain and Portugal had preserved the integrity of their conscientious conservatism and how far they would be prepared to welcome closer collaboration with the countries beyond the Pyrenees. It was twenty-five years since I had last visited Jerez and Oporto, and I feared that in that momentous quarter of a century much of the old tradition of wine-making and the scrupulous attention to detail which the making of good wine necessitates might have been submerged by the commercial temptations of mass production.

My fears were vain. The loyalty to ancient custom was less surprising in Spain than in Portugal; for Spain after a

Civil War which cost her a million dead was poorer than she had ever been, and it is wealth that corrupts the good manners of more than wine-growers. In Jerez I discovered that the ritual of Sherry-making had undergone no more change than that which was admitted in the laws of the Medes and Persians. About half way between my visits, a leading wine-grower had expended a very considerable sum in the purchase of the most up-to-date machinery, to deal with his grape juice, his *mostos*, and his finished wines, in accordance with the latest scientific principles. Naturally he expected wonderful things from the vintage that followed its installation. There was nothing wrong with the weather —there rarely is in Jerez—and his grape harvest seemed first rate, but for some inexplicable reason his wine was not up to standard. He could only suppose that the new machinery needed getting used to and that his men had handled it badly. The same disappointment awaited him in the following year; again his wines were inferior to those produced by growers whom in the past he had not deigned to look upon as competitors. The failure of the third vintage put an end once and for all to his experiment in modernity. All his scientific gadgets were sold and the primitive traditions of the past were restored. Once again men trod the grapes in raw-hide boots with soles heavily nailed, the nails arranged in such a pattern as not to break the pips, once again the mash of trodden grapes was built into a cylinder round the centre screw of the wine press and held in place by swathing round it *à la* Heath Robinson puttees of esparto matting, once again pressure was applied to it by human muscles, a grunting gang working on long levers like capstan bars, which were as elastic and sensitive in their operation as a machine could never be. Since this revolution of reaction, his wines have resumed their wonted place at the head of their kind and have never looked back.

We have been singularly unwise on our efforts to teach Spain how she should be governed and as five centuries ago she craved for world domination, so now her main concern is to be left alone in the isolation of her own thoughts. On the day the United Nations made up their minds that sending Spain to Coventry was a profitless gesture, a young Spaniard over several *copitas* of Fino Sherry expounded to me the Spanish point of view. "European politics," he said, "will never mean much to us, for it is our fate to be a protest against Europe." He adumbrated with a finger on the café table a map of the Peninsula. "We stand or fall," he went on, "by our faith in things spiritual; beyond the Pyrenees only things material count. Spain is the country of *espiritualismo*, and poverty and spirituality go hand in hand. We shall always be poor, and you may think us mad for accepting poverty. Indeed we are mad, and always everything we say or do will cry out against the materialism of Europe."

Such an attitude appeared of little encouragement for my scheme of an European Union, but Sherry was a link between us and *espiritualismo* was no bar to favouring an extension of the Sherry trade in the materialist world. French wines were of necessity the first to find a market in our islands, but by Chaucer's time Spanish wines had begun to challenge their supremacy. As has been said, white wines from Lepe Southern Spain some forty miles from Niebla are mentioned by the Pardoner in *The Canterbury Tales* as an exceptionally intoxicating beverage and as blending wines fraudulently used to give unnatural strength to wines of Gascony. The wine of Lepe is dry but not particularly strong, and I feel sure Manuel Gonzalez is right when he hazards the guess that Chaucer's Lepe wine was fortified. The Spaniards knew all about distillation from the Moors. There is every reason to believe that the popularity of Sack was largely due to the added spirit. It was apart from the very expensive dessert wines the only wine that would keep, as is shown by the regular cry for *Old Sack* at a time when new wines were rated higher than old wines which were generally going bad. Apart from what I believe to be the mistaken derivation of Sack from *seco*, *dry*, there is no evidence that Sack was in any respect a dry wine. The earliest quotation for its use given in the *Oxford English Dictionary* comes from an Act of Henry VIII dated 1531-2 controlling the price of Malmseys, Romaneys, "Sakkes," and "other swete wynes." Who can doubt that Falstaff would have scorned dry wines as thin potations? I am convinced that Sack has nothing to do with *seco*, but that it stands for the word *saca*, the technical word for the export of Jerez wines and still used in that sense. *Sacar* means *to take out* and *vinos de saca* were the wines made at Jerez for export. If they were so described by the English importers, it was almost inevitable that Sack should be connected with the familiar French *sec*. Sack then might be brought forward as a historic slogan proclaiming alliance between Britain and Spain.

There was, I believed, more danger that Portugal might have been led astray and followed shoddy new notions instead of the established golden rule, since wealth had been her lot in these latter years. It was a relief to find no basic change. Up the Douro there were still Quintas that could only be reached by foot, horse-back or ox cart, and there was no question of the wine-farmer dispensing with his oxen, beasts of burden of a race apart, or with the un-greased wheels of his carts that screech to high heaven to announce their approach along the narrow tracks. Salazar, the dictator, who I am disposed to think is the only philosopher king the world has ever known—his one desire is to return to his professorship in the University of Coimbra—is blessed with a genius for letting well alone. He sees no reason why the peasant who feels no itch for book learning should have it forced upon him, and the idea of the higher education of the Douro bullock has not entered his head as it surely would have done if he had been an Anglo-Saxon. As it is, these oxen have never been taught to feed themselves and entirely depend for their nourishment on the ministrations of an urchin, one urchin to each yoke of bullocks, who feeds them by hand and never leaves them by day or night; for their meals must be regular and frequent, and they suffer from night starvation.

All the gay trimmings of the vintage that make Port such a happy wine, the ritual dances of the treading, the polishing of the master's shoes when he comes into the place of the wine-press, the wolf howls of the men carrying the grapes down mountain paths in great baskets that hang between their shoulders with the weight supported by a strap across their brow—all the legendary mirth of Bacchus has been preserved and in the making of the wine there has been no innovation that can affect its excellence. The exigencies of war compelled the shippers to bottle their vintage wines in Oporto instead of sending them to Britain as soon as they were ready to be free of the wood, but this expedient was not entirely a novelty, since there had always been vintage wines bottled in their home for their shippers to drink in Portugal. It is true that opinions are not entirely agreed as to the advantages and disadvantages of the Oporto bottling, but the wines I tasted appeared to have developed well and normally.

The grand old tradition of the eighteenth-century Factory House is maintained and on Wednesdays a memorable luncheon gathers together the leading lights of the Port trade in the true style of the Merchant Prince. A minor and interesting innovation I noted. In the old days before the meal only Sherry was served in the palatial antechamber to the dining-room, but now the Sherry decanter is flanked by a decanter of dry white Port. This white Port aspires to the place of an *apéritif*, and though it is too strong and full of flavour to make a fitting introduction to fine and delicate wines, if any such be offered with the repast, yet if no good wine is forthcoming, and some such beverage of austerity as iced water is the order of the day, then it serves admirably to brace the system and steel the heart to endure through the trial of food unsublimated by good wine until the end, when surely patience and courage should be rewarded by one or more glasses of noble red Port.

My Wine Utopia of Western Europe can count on the wholehearted support of Portugal; not for nothing has that country boasted itself our oldest ally and wine is consecrated as our bond of union by the treaty that makes the title of Port sacrosanct. There is as good wine to be had in Portugal as ever there was, and the wine-lover so far as Nature and the art of winemaking are concerned would find in France, Spain and Portugal no shortage of the material to make glad his heart, if it were not for the curse of politics and the irremediable folly of the human race which splits the world, with the lightness of heart with which it splits the atom, into a melancholy honeycomb of uncommunicating cells.

INDEX

WINE WRITING AT ITS FINEST

ON BORDEAUX
Tales of the Unexpected from the World's Greatest Wine Region
Susan Keevil
Why these wines are the most talked-about.

CHATEAU MUSAR
The Story of a Wine Icon
Serge Hochar and the most famous wine to come out of Lebanon.

IN VINO VERITAS
A Collection of Fine Wine Writing, Past and Present
Susan Keevil
The quintessential browsing book for those who love wine.

STEVEN SPURRIER
A Life in Wine
The incidents, adventures, ideas and discoveries that formed a remarkable wine journey.

THE STORY OF WINE
From Noah to Now
Hugh Johnson
The new edition of Hugh Johnson's captivating journey through wine history.

SHERRY
Maligned, Misunderstood, Magnificent!
Ben Howkins
This sun-drenched wine returns to our lives with a flourish.

WINE TASTING
Commemorative Edition
Michael Broadbent
The definitive guide that began it all.

10 GREAT WINE FAMILIES
A Tour Through Europe
Fiona Morrison MW
An up-close and personal insight into Europe's most celebrated winemaking families.

VIKING IN THE VINEYARD
Stories from a Revolutionary Winemaker
Peter Vinding-Diers
Six decades of wine adventure: Peter's pioneering exploits from Stellenbosch to Sicily.

OZ CLARKE ON WINE
Your Global Wine Companion
A fast-paced tour of the world's most delicious wine styles with Oz.

ON CALIFORNIA
From Napa to Nebbiolo… Wine Tales from the Golden State
Susan Keevil
California's great wine adventure as told by our A-list team of experts and enthusiasts.

CLASSIC EDITIONS
WAYWARD TENDRILS OF THE VINE
Ian Maxwell Campbell
An affectionate glimpse back to the Golden Age of wine. (1948)

IN THE VINE COUNTRY
Edith Somerville & Martin Ross
Anglo-Irish cousins and writing companions set out on a harvest-time journey through the vineyards of Bordeaux. (1893)

STAY ME WITH FLAGONS
Maurice Healy
A love letter to wine from a brilliant Irish raconteur. (1940)

www.academieduvinlibrary.com